GARDEN BOUQUETS AND BEYOND

Garden Bouquets and Beyond

Creating Wreaths, Garlands, and More in Every Garden Season

Suzy Bales

FOREWORD BY DR. ALLAN M. ARMITAGE

PHOTOGRAPHS BY STEVEN RANDAZZO

Rodale books may be purchased for business or promotional use or for special sales.
For information, please write to:
Special Markets Department, Rodale Inc., 733 Third Avenue, New York, NY 10017.

Printed in the United States of America
Rodale Inc. makes every effort to use acid-free ♾, recycled paper ♾.

Book design by Doug Turshen with David Huang
All photographs by Steven Randazzo except for the following: page 187 top right by Carter Bales;
pages xiii, 2, 12, 26, 34, 37, 45, 47, 48-49, 54-55, 57-58, 65-68, 72-73, 77 left, 78, 88-89, 91, 92,
94, 96, 99, 107, 111 top left, 111 bottom right, 112-114, 115 left, 116-120, 124-127, 140, 143 right, 147 left,
151, 157, 159, 161, 170, 174, and 199-205 by Suzy Bales; page 187 bottom left by Bridget Gallagher;
page 63 by Richard Klemm; pages 90 and 187 bottom left by Michael Luppino; pages ix, 7, 9, 36,
39, and 61 by Robert Starkoff; pages 40, 62, and 98 by Richard Warren

ON THE COVER: A wicker plant stand holds a bouquet of
assorted peonies and roses arranged in floral foam.
OPPOSITE: A floral foam wreath covered in pachysandra, assorted roses,
and clematis 'Betty Corning' welcomes guests at the garden gate.

Library of Congress Cataloging-in-Publication Data

Bales, Suzanne Frutig.
    Garden bouquets and beyond : creating wreaths, garlands, and more in every garden season /
Suzy Bales ; foreword by Allan Armitage ; photographs by Steven Randazzo.
        p.   cm.
    Includes index.
    ISBN-13: 978-1-60529-010-2   hardcover
    ISBN-10: 1-60529-010-6   hardcover
    1. Floral decorations.   2. Plants, Ornamental—Seasonal variations.   I. Randazzo, Steven.
II. Title.
SB449.B244   2010
745.92—dc22   2009038916

Distributed to the trade by Macmillan
2   4   6   8   10   9   7   5   3   1   hardcover

We inspire and enable people to improve their lives and the world around them
For more of our products visit **rodalestore.com** or call 800-848-4735

To Doug Turshen:
An extraordinary designer,
a supportive friend,
and a wise mentor

Contents

'Mr. Lincoln', a fragrant hybrid tea rose, marches down the center of the table, each large bloom in its own glass—a party favor for guests to take home.

FOREWORD

I have always been impressed with Suzy Bales's work and writing, and I knew that if she were going to write a book on floral arranging, it would come from her heart and equally important, from her garden. Yet when I was asked to introduce her book, I almost declined. After all, while I enjoy good floral design, there seemed to be more than enough books, papers, and words written on the subject. But Suzy offers something many of the others don't—she is every woman's (and every man's) answer to bringing the garden inside to soften the house when friends come over or more important, simply for the sheer joy of it!

She quickly makes us realize that we don't need an excuse to bring flowers (or stems, leaves, buds, and berries) into our homes; simple arrangements are for everyone, even those of us who would rather relax with a cup of tea than entertain. She also makes it simple to do this stuff. After all, we don't have to create bodacious bouquets for the White House or the Boston Pops. I make no apologies about my lack of flower-arranging talent, but I know that when I pick flowers from my garden, I feel like an expert. Suzy shows simple ways to combine plants already in our gardens that even made me believe I could create something inviting and comfortable.

There are many facets about this book I enjoy but a number quickly stand out. I am a gardener and I appreciate the fact that all her bouquets are from her own garden; that makes the gardener in me turn page after page to see what else she is growing. I love how she plants for four-season interest and extols everything from twigs to bulbs to colorful shrubs in the bouquets. I love how she invites me to walk through her garden and enjoy it from January to December. For me, this is a garden book and an arrangement book all in one!

When I cut and arrange stems, I would like them to last for more than a day. As a scientist and researcher in the production and postharvest of cut flowers, it is refreshing to find facts based on actual data, and even more enlightening to read about the myths and misconceptions that result in short vase life. While the proper cutting and handling of cut flowers from the garden is not brain surgery, Suzy captures all of the fine details and makes the science easy to understand and immediately useful. How invigorating is that?

I could go on and on about the beautiful writing, the seasonal organization, the useful vase life chart and, of course, the brilliant photos, but start turning the pages and get into the good stuff. It is not an easy task to write a book; authors vacillate, struggle with words, question their sanity, and test their commitment, but in the end, they hope that others will celebrate what they have written. I, for one, am raising a glass to Suzy, her garden, and her bouquets. Well done.

–Dr. Allan M. Armitage

A Chinese basket holds an arrangement of zinnias, balloon flower, cosmos, ageratum, tobacco plant, blue salvia, and love-in-a-puff.

Pink and yellow English roses along with purple 'Jackmanii' and blue 'General Sikorski' clematis are a compatible mix in the vase and in the garden.

INTRODUCTION

I think of flowers the way most people think of money; there can never be enough! Flowers are such joyful creatures, such living marvels of nature. They share their joy with everyone who touches them or leans in for a whiff. So I'm always looking for more creative ways to keep them close at hand. The pleasure of arranging flowers, as well as the joy that comes from giving them to others, is addicting. The next time you offer a garden bouquet to someone, watch their face change as they receive it. If they bury their nose in the blooms, you have stirred a kindred spirit and made a friend for life.

Bringing bouquets from my garden into my home breaks the barrier between inside and out. It opens a window on nature's astonishing world and imparts a special wisdom that only increases the more you do it. Flowers and foliage from one's own garden are different from those at the market. They are not as perfect, it's true—but they are real and honest creatures, with no pretense.

Flowers are marvels we cannot begin to understand. Yet too many of us take flowers for granted, missing the splendors and mysteries of nature. Ever wonder what causes the design on the petal of a checkered lily or why cleome stems are sticky? What protects delicate petals from the rain? How winter bloomers push through the frozen earth, lifting their heads above the snow? I've noticed a blue sweet-pea petal stains whatever it touches when it is wet—hands, clothes, and tablecloths. A pink or red one leaves no mark. How curious, how wondrous!

A cutting garden is not necessary for making bouquets. More important, look closer at what is already around you; you have more to pick than you think. The trick is to stop categorizing everything as a flower, tree, vine, seed head, or shrub and to look anew to see if it has an interesting shape or color. I cut indiscriminately from any plant, anywhere—container gardens, flower borders, foundation plantings, vegetable gardens, and the roadside when no one is looking.

I've never been concerned with flower trends, nor have I snubbed common flowers. Well, maybe that one time when I tossed out gladiolas, but I swear that's it. In fact, it's quite the opposite. I admire common flowers; the more common, the better. Such plants give uncommonly of themselves and deserve to be sainted, not shunned.

This book starts with the seasons of my adventures, exploring the garden all year through. It is only a beginning. So many plants, even ones I adore, are not included

simply because of space limitations. My apologies to the flowers that didn't make it into the book. What can I say? Things happen!

In "Tricks of the Trade," I explain the basics for harvesting flowers, prolonging their blooms, and making bouquets and all things beyond—from wreaths, garlands, and mock topiaries to candle cups and toppings for gifts. These designs can be repeated with different flowers and foliage. Mastering the technical skills is easy. Start simply. Then jump-start your self-expression. You're the artist. Do it your way!

A round wire wreath form is covered in oak, maple, and forsythia leaves with crabapples poked in. A sunflower seed head and shafts of wheat complete the design.

BELOW: Long stems of 'America', a fragrant red peony, are poked in among the branches of a pink rosebud azalea. OPPOSITE: Looking closely at the arrangement makes it easy to see that the azalea blooms resemble rosebuds.

PART 1

Seasonal Gathering from the Garden

A basket of early spring snippings includes purple and green hellebores, golden daffodils, red species tulips, burgundy dwarf iris, and purple, pink, and white hyacinths.

Spring's Awakening

When the daffodils bloom, I'm as invigorated and happy as a child with a pocketful of change at the candy store. Daffodils signal that spring has burst out of winter's corset, a charming reason to welcome them into your garden. Once the daffodils dance on the hillsides, the spring parade of flowers marches in. Generally, spring blooms are in bright crayon colors that can hold their own against the others, so I let the flowers I cut almost arrange themselves. I break all of my own rules of flower design and throw everything into an arrangement. But isn't that what rules are for—to break?

SPRING FAVORITES AT A GLANCE

Spring is a season of strong, quick growth culminating in radical changes in the garden from one week to the next. Since most change is led by the colorful parade of blossoming bulbs, I continually look for more places to plant them. I tuck them into nooks and crannies, open lawn, under cover of trees, and among sleeping perennials. They bring cheer wherever they bloom, then disappear quickly to lend the ground to the later-flowering perennials and annuals. In my list of favorite spring plants, I have only touched on a few of the flowering trees and shrubs that bloom in spring. There are so many more that you'll enjoy seeking out.

FLOWERS

Azalea (*Rhododendron* species)

Bishop's hat (*Epimedium grandiflorum*)

Bleeding heart (*Dicentra spectabilis*)

Bluebell, English (*Hyacinthoides non-scripta*)

Bluebell, Spanish (*Hyacinthoides hispanica*)

Bluebell, Virginia (*Mertensia virginica*)

Cherries, ornamental (*Prunus* sp.)

Clematis (*Clematis* sp. and cultivars)

Cowslip (*Primula veris*)

Crabapples (*Malus* cvs.)

Daffodils (*Narcissus* sp. and cvs.)

Dogwood (*Cornus* cvs.)

Forsythia (*Forsythia* x *intermedia*)

Glory of the snow (*Chionodoxa luciliae*)

Hyacinth (*Hyacinthus orientalis*)

Hyacinth, grape (*Muscari* sp.)

Iris (*Iris* sp. and hybrids)

Lilacs (*Syringa vulgaris*)

Lilacs, Preston (*Syringa* x *prestoniae*)

Lily, trout (*Erythronium americanum*)

Lily-of-the-valley (*Convallaria majalis*)

Peonies (*Paeonia* cvs.)

Peony, tree (*Paeonia suffruticosa*)

Rhododendron (*Rhododendron* hybrids)

Snowflakes (*Leucojum* sp.)

Solomon's seal, variegated (*Polygonatum odoratum* 'Variegatum')

Tulips (*Tulipa* sp. and hybrids)

Viburnum (*Viburnum* cvs.)

Wisteria (Wisteria sp.)

Winter hazel, spike (*Corylopsis spicata*)

A copper pot hanging on the garden gate holds Virginia bluebells, assorted daffodils, and snowflakes. The flowers stayed fresh for more than a week in the cool spring air.

GET THE JOINT A-JUMPIN'

As the woods awake from their long winter sleep, I clip a collection of the returning perennials and bulbs and bring them in to celebrate the life cycle of the garden. The clippings don't lend themselves to an arrangement, yet each placed in its own vase and then grouped together brings indoors the message that the garden is awakening from its winter nap. I find it fascinating how fern fronds stretch up like curled fingers. And I can't resist the trout lilies in white and yellow, miniature versions of summer's Oriental lilies—they seem to be heralding what is to come. Bishop's hat waves in the breeze as I pass. So many delicate tiny flowers line its airy stems that I have to cut a few. Snowflakes and hellebores are the transition team, easily moving from late winter to spring to join in the merriment.

Spring is the original quick-change artist; each week is so different from the next as the marathon of bloomers races by. Bulbs carry the season along smoothly and offer lush color to bouquets. By planting spring bulbs that reliably return, your blooms multiply year after year. Let the natural beauty of bulbs shine by clustering them in groups—whether in the garden or in the vase. A generous grouping of stems in your hand spreads out naturally in a vase. Of course, the smaller the bulb, the more stems you'll need to make a statement.

OPPOSITE: A collection of bottles holds white and yellow trout lilies, a red and yellow species tulip, orange bishop's cap, white snowflakes, green fern fronds, and green hellebores.
BELOW: A handful of individual bloomers— daffodils, dwarf iris, tulips, pansies, glory of the snow, crocus, and hyacinths—each in its own glass basket.

The champions of spring, daffodils and tulips, turn up in courtyards as well as country meadows. Have you noticed that there are so many other spring bloomers that are just as pretty, yet not as well known? Grape hyacinth, hyacinth, bluebells, checkered lilies, and snowflakes all have easygoing ways and a tendency to return year after year. They are worth the investment.

DAFFY FOR DAFFODILS

Daffodils, the large and gifted Narcissus family, are among the most self-sufficient bulbs. A plethora of daffodils in different sizes and shapes and with different bloom times brightens spring from late March to mid-May. Although it is easy to identify a "daff," there are so many variations, running the gamut from large trumpet flowers with swept-back petals to double flowers that form rosettes rather than trumpets. And then there is the distinct and powerfully scented pheasant's-eye (*Narcissus* 'Actaea'). This is similar to a dogwood bloom with large white petals surrounding a small, red-rimmed yellow cup. Daffodil colors vary, too, from all white or yellow to mixtures with orange or pink. But all daffodils have stiff, straight, hollow stems—which means a bouquet, tied at the neck, can stand up on its own. This makes it a cinch to carry a cluster to a friend or to ship a bouquet.

Opposite: Daffodils increase yearly, yielding lots for picking, while tulips need to be replanted every few years. Below: A bunch of daffodils tied with a ribbon is an easy-to-give gift from the garden.

I've sent armloads of daffodils to my parents in Florida for half the price of ordering from a florist. Living in Florida, my parents miss seeing them in the garden. I condition the daffodils (see page 191) before shipping them via overnight delivery, coddled in plastic bubble wrap. I always let my folks know when the flowers are coming, so they can put them in water immediately. (Most longer-lasting flowers ship easily out of water.) Although I have nothing against shipping flowers from a florist or mail-order source, a bouquet from your own garden is much more personal, and you have the pleasure of knowing exactly what your recipient is getting. There are no disappointments with this kind of gift!

The most desirable daffodils trumpet the season with a lovely perfume. Scentless daffs are in the majority, however, so choose carefully for sweetly scented ones. With careful selection, it is possible to plant successive scented

varieties for a 3-month perfumed display. A few favorites to consider for season-long scent include Queen Anne's double jonquil (*Narcissus* 'Albus Plenus Odoratus'), 'Trevithian', and 'Tête-à-Tête' for early bloom; 'Carlton', 'Big Gun', and 'Baby Moon' for mid-season; and 'Sir Winston Churchill', 'Yellow Cheerfulness', and 'Thalia' as a finale.

Fragrance aside, it is impossible not to be infatuated with many other unique characters in the Narcissus family. 'Peeping Tom' and 'Nosie Posie' lead by a nose with long yellow but, alas, scentless snouts. 'Avalanche' is a bouquet in itself with from 3 to 20 flowers to a stem, and 'Baby Moon' has several scented, nickel-size golden yellow flowers per stem. All of these stand out in arrangements.

OPPOSITE: A bouquet of tulips, checkered lilies, cowslips, hyacinths, bleeding hearts, and daffodils is poked into floral foam hidden by a basket. BELOW: Daffodils, winter hazel, and hellebores are arranged in floral foam in an ice bucket.

I plant for a long progression of daffodils with early, mid-, and late-season bloomers. The first daffodils, usually 'February Gold', open in March and integrate well with winter hazel, hellebores, and a little later with forsythia. Then mid-season daffs open up to complement hyacinths and tulips. Within a few weeks, there will be late-blooming daffs to welcome the lilacs and peonies. In fact, there isn't any flower that daffodils don't flatter. Despite their charms, though, daffodils ooze a toxic sap when they're cut. In a vase, this sap mixed in the water can clog the stems of other flowers. (In the garden, the sap serves a good purpose: It keeps deer and other pests away.) So you must be sure to first condition the daffs by placing them in their own container of water for 6 hours or overnight before transferring them to a vase with other blossoms. Or, keep the daffs in their own vase but position it with a mix of other containers. I often group several glass baskets together, each holding its own family of flowers.

TULIPOMANIA

Tulips are the most popular flowers of spring. It might be because they can be had in so many different colors—from cotton-candy pink to "punks" in purple and orange flames. Whatever your mood, they'll make it better.

If I had lived in the 16th century during *Tulipomania*, when single tulip bulbs were selling for more than the price of a house, I might have traded my house for a tulip, too. Today, thank goodness, we can all own hundreds of the Rembrandt tulips that caused all the fuss and keep our houses as well. These spectacular flowers, familiar subjects in Dutch paintings, are flamed with scarlet, plum, white, bronzy yellow, and cream. Looking back, one can understand how such uncommon beauty made ordinary people do crazy things.

Opposite: An urn outfitted with floral foam holds a formal arrangement of tulips, daffodils, azaleas, flowering quince, and hyacinths. Below: Yawning tulips are combined with *Kerria japonica*, lilacs, and daffodils in a glass vase.

Tulips are still pricey compared with daffodils and most are not likely to return after a few years, although there are exceptions. Darwin hybrid tulips in single colors are often sold as "perennial tulips," because they return consistently year after year in the garden. We have had solid yellow ones for decades. They were planted by my husband in the sandy, well-draining soil at the edge of the beach and they are very content. Even those that don't reliably return, I rationalize, are cheaper by a long shot to plant and enjoy for a few years than to buy a bouquet of them as cut flowers.

Some of the unique tulips are worth seeking out. 'Queen of Night', with its deep purple cup, is one of the last to bloom. It has reappeared at our place for more than a decade. Oddly enough, this tulip is more effective in a cut arrangement than in the garden, adding depth and interest to a bouquet with its dark purple, almost black, color. I love to partner it with the white-edged purple blooms of the lilac 'Sensation.' For a different look entirely, pair 'Orange Parrot', a deliciously fragrant tulip cultivar with flared petals that resemble a parrot's wing, with lilacs in a vase. The tulips positively jump out and dance against the purple of the lilac sprays.

Species tulips are not as well known as their hybrid cousins but they are more likely to naturalize. Plant them once, and they'll show up yearly for a decade or more if they are happily situated. The first dividends arrive as early as late March when species tulips combine with daffodils and early spring bulbs. A favorite species tulip is *Tulipa clusiana*. If multiple nicknames are a sign of love, then this one is adored by many gardeners. Quite popular in long-ago times, you still can ask for it by several common names: lady tulip, candy tulip, and peppermint-stick tulip. Alas, it isn't grown much now but it should be! Among the oldest tulips in cultivation, it was first discovered in a garden in 1606. Named for the botanist Carolus Clusius, who did much to popularize his find in Europe, this pretty tulip has long narrow flowers with candy-striped white petals. It's

long blooming, reaches 8 to 12 inches high, and has a heavenly fragrance. It has been returning in my garden for a decade or more. A sister cultivar, 'Cynthia', bears creamy-yellow flowers with red stripes. Although species tulips are slightly shorter with smaller flowers than the hybrid tulips, these qualities become assets when plants are artfully mingled in the garden or the vase with other smaller, early-blooming bulbs such as checkered lilies (*Fritillaria meleagris*), hyacinths, and daffodils.

If you've planted early, mid-, and late-season varieties, hybrid tulips continue blooming through May and can enliven lilacs and early roses in the vase. The red-and-white striped double tulip, 'Semper Maxima', makes quite a show when combined with all-white flowers of two different varieties of lilacs. 'Angélique' is another double tulip beauty with pink flowers, especially pretty with pink lilacs.

OPPOSITE: White lilacs are the perfect backdrop for the gorgeous, late-blooming 'Semper Maxima' tulips. ABOVE: Lilac 'Sensation' combines beautifully with purple azalea and orange tulips.

Strangely, tulip stems continue to grow an inch or two in the vase, even after they are cut. They also relax into curves rather than standing ramrod straight like daffodils. That is why some florists wire them to sticks to keep their posture. I prefer to let them loose, loving their curves. Even indoors, tulips open and close with the light. If the light is bright, the tulip opens its mouth so far that it looks like it is yawning. This can throw the balance off in a bouquet but it really doesn't matter: If you look into the mouth of a tulip, you notice nothing else.

CHASING THE BLUES

Blue is a favorite color in the garden as it easily combines with all others. I do plant as many easy-care blues as I can find. Pansies, when planted out in fall, will bloom in early spring and keep going into early summer until the high temperatures drive them away. If winter is mild, they might make their faces known as early as late winter. Their short stems necessitate tiny arrangements, so I tuck pansies into mini vases and at Easter into colored eggshells.

Among the earliest spring bulbs, there is an array of blue bloomers like glory of the snow, scilla, crocus, and dwarf iris that spans the season from winter to spring, when grape hyacinth, hyacinth, and English, Spanish, and Virginia bluebells appear.

Grape hyacinth is my garden's sentinel, standing at attention in its small peaked cap, all the while perfuming the air around it. It comes in many different guises, from the most common, *Muscari armeniacum*, all dressed in blue, to *M. latifolium*, with its two tiers of flowers—the bottom one violet and the top bright blue. On their short stems, grape hyacinths fill smaller containers beautifully.

When Easter comes early in April, I assemble a basket resembling a bird's nest filled with assorted hardboiled eggs and broken empty eggshells all dyed robin's-

A LITTLE HOUSEKEEPING

All bulbs benefit from having their flowers cut. Harvesting blossoms halts the production of seeds, so energy is conserved for the next season's blooms. Be careful, however, to take as few leaves as possible. Foliage is needed to replenish the bulb with stored food and to form the embryo for next year's flowers. Once the embryo flower is formed, the bulb's foliage ripens and decays. Only then should the foliage be removed.

egg blue. I poke a handful of grape hyacinths and a few little 'February Gold' daffodils into a dyed eggshell filled with a spoonful of wet floral foam. Lungwort, *Pulmonaria* 'Mrs. Moon', an early-blooming shade perennial with its blue and pink flowers and spotted leaves, easily fits into another eggshell. Glory of the snow and dwarf iris pop out of others. If pussy willows are blooming, I weave some of their blossoms into the basket as a bird might do, making it more eye-catching.

Traditional hyacinths are just as formal, upright, and rigid as grape hyacinths but they're much larger. I must admit I find them difficult to arrange. They have been hybridized to be so top-heavy that they remind me of overdressed floozies tottering down the street on high heels. Sometimes, to scent the room, I tuck one in the back of an arrangement where it hardly shows. Other times I give hyacinths their own vase. One Easter I cut a stem of deep purple hyacinth into smaller pieces and poked them into a floral foam wreath around the neck of a garden rabbit. Daffodils, winter hazel, and glory of the snow completed the effect. Mr. Rabbit sat on the front porch and greeted the family when they came for dinner. It could just as easily have been the dinner table's centerpiece.

OPPOSITE: An iron bunny wears a wreath of daffodils, glory of the snow, hyacinths, and winter hazel. BELOW: Easter eggs and eggshells filled with flowers nestle in a basket woven with pussy willows.

Fortunately, each year hyacinths return with fewer and fewer blossoms, eventually reverting to their ancestors' stature, with fewer individual blooms so each blossom is seen and not squashed between others. What's more, the once too stiff stems gently curve for a more graceful effect. But one thing that does not change is the perfume. Hyacinths' strong scent is reminiscent of a plum pie baked with cloves and topped with sugar and cinnamon. Like other powerful floral perfumes, the hyacinth fragrance is deep and evocative, composed of many unidentifiable notes.

BELLS ARE RINGING

A number of different flowers answer to the picturesque title of bluebell. I recommend three different ones—English, Spanish, and Virginia. All of these bluebells multiply freely, naturalizing to form impressive colonies, and bloom for 4 to 6 weeks without giving much trouble. Each of them mixes effortlessly with daffodils or other spring blooms in the garden and the vase. If the English and the Spanish bluebells are planted near each other, they often readily hybridize with interesting results.

OPPOSITE: Virginia bluebells and purple hyacinths bloom above a rectangular glass vase. BELOW: Teddy, my West Highland terrier, peeks out from under the table.

The English bluebell is a bulb admired for its sweet scent and modest demeanor. From 6 to 12 narrow flowers, just ¼ inch to ½ inch long, dangle from one side of its stem, causing it to dip demurely at the top, as though chastened by its own beauty. Inside each tiny bloom are cream-colored anthers that make the flower look like a graceful gong. Although there are pink and white varieties, it is the blue version that can make my heart skip a beat when it romps under trees, runs down a woodland path, or is bunched in a vase with tulips and daffodils.

ISN'T IT OBVIOUS?

It's official! Living with flowers is soothing. A 2006 Harvard study concluded what gardeners and floral designers have always known: Spending time in the company of flowers lifts your spirits. It's the floral equivalent of a big hug. Nancy L. Etcoff, a clinical researcher in psychology at Harvard Medical School, asked 55 women to keep diaries recording their daily activities and emotions for 2 weeks. When she surprised them with bouquets of flowers, she discovered that with each delivery, the flowers produced positive emotions in the women over the next few days. She also noted that having flowers in the home heightened the women's feelings of relaxation, energy, and compassion for others. All in all, the study had a firm grasp of the obvious. Gardeners have always known flowers lift spirits!

Perhaps to make up for the fact that it is a scentless bulb, the Spanish bluebell (*Hyacinthoides hispanica* and *Scilla hispanica*) boasts a sturdier, taller, more upright stem than its English cousin, with as many as 15 open blossoms in pink, blue, or white and glossy dark green leaves. In all of these the anthers are blue.

The Virginia bluebell is not a bulb, although it behaves like one, dying back after it finishes its bloom. It is an easygoing and unpretentious native perennial. It first opens with pink nodding bells that change to blue over its long month or two of bloom. Its sky blue color always contains hints of purple and pink. In bouquets, it brightens all the other flowers. A grouping of delicate Virginia bluebells and tulips is always a hit, as one dangles down and the other is upright. I've greeted guests with a large bunch of daffodils and Virginia bluebells hanging in a copper pot on the orchard gate (see page 5). I also like the gently curving stems of Virginia bluebells mixed with the straighter stems of hyacinth—a blue-on-blue combination that sings.

(see page 5)

I do caution you that as soon as Virginia bluebells are picked, they begin to wilt. It is necessary to remove all their leaves and condition them overnight in a refrigerator or cool place (a shady outdoor spot often works) to revive them. Then they will continue for several days.

OPPOSITE: An all-white arrangement of different shapes and sizes of flowers goes anywhere. This spring bouquet includes snowflakes, checkered lilies, and 'Erlicheer' and 'Ice Wings' daffodils.

REMINDERS OF WINTER SNOW

The 2-foot-high "summer" snowflake (*Leucojum aestivum*) has four to eight white bells tipped in green dangling from each stem. Despite its common name, the chocolate-scented snowflake actually blossoms in spring. The tallest is 'Gravetye Giant'. He hangs around for a good long while. The only criticism I've heard is that he multiplies too fast, but I count that as a blessing. Snowflakes disappear quickly without unsightly dying foliage, so what's the problem? I let them roam our woods. In bouquets, snowflakes fit in anywhere.

COWSLIPS

Most primroses bloom on short stems—but not the cowslip, an English native wildflower. It stands tall and straight at 1 to 2 feet, topped by whorls of yellow flowers. Each plant sends up multiple stems over a 6-week period, so there are lots for picking. I started off with a small clump at one side of a massive oak and after I divided them yearly, they now encircle the tree.

When combining cowslips with other woodland bloomers in a rustic basket, a little of this and a little of that can be beguiling. Poked into a concealed bowl of floral foam, variegated Solomon's seal sets the shape of the bouquet with outstretched arms jingling white bells. A few wisteria blooms spill out in front, softening the edge of the basket as they perfume the air. The bright blues of Spanish and English bluebells perk up the mix, and a few late daffodils add a touch more fragrance. One lonely yellow-and-green tulip acts as the focal point.

LILY-OF-THE-VALLEY

Locked in the scent of lily-of-the-valley is the memory of my grandmother's garden and the large bouquet she picked for me to take to my kindergarten teacher. As I rode in the car, I remember burying my nose in the blooms to inhale the exquisite perfume. The traditional way to display this winsome charmer is in a nosegay of flower stems encircled with leaves. It is simple to attach it to the top of a present or to plunk it into a vase (see page 32). Lily-of-the-valley also melds well with the bell-shaped blossoms of bluebells and grape hyacinth. In my opinion, blue-and-white bouquets fit in anywhere.

When lily-of-the-valley first appears, its leaves pierce through the cold earth scrolled tightly around the waxy white bells. I find myself wondering whether this flower is simply shy or whether it's protecting its beguiling perfume from the damp and cold. How do such tiny blooms exhale so intense an aroma? It's nature's secret, I realize, and I feel privileged to breathe in the spiciness. For thrill seekers, there is a pink lily-of-the-valley, *Convallaria majalis* var. *rosea*. But for me, it wears too much rouge; I prefer the delicate white version. I don't have to worry about deer eating these when they've exhausted many other food sources; lily-of-the-valley is poisonous and the deer leave it alone.

A large twig basket outfitted with floral foam holds a mixture of variegated Solomon's seal, daffodils, cowslips, snowflakes, viburnum, wisteria, hyacinths, and columbine circling around a tulip.

SCENE STEALERS

The checkered lily *(Fritillaria meleagris)* is a most remarkable bulb. Each stem is topped with a drooping purple-and-white checkered bell (or sometimes two). Its intricate pattern is a fascinating checkerboard design superbly mottled in muted shades of bronze, purple, and white. Each bell is a show-off no matter what other flowers are nearby. Once seen, it isn't easily forgotten. Happily, the checkered lily is not only inexpensive; it colonizes easily and sets up shop for a prolonged stay.

These exotic beauties are so unique that they need to be seen up close in an arrangement. When propped against the white or soft pink blooms of flowering ornamental cherry branches, the dark bells stand out in relief. If I mix them in with other colors, their darker color tends to recede, so I prop their nodding bells to "ring out" over the edge of the container, where they are seen in silhouette.

OPPOSITE: Checkered lilies appear to be jumping out of the vase of cherry blossoms. BELOW: 'Sensation' lilacs, orange parrot tulips, daffodils, bleeding heart, and black 'Queen of the Night' tulips all clash together among the fallen cherry blossoms.

Here's a bonus: If you buy a mix of checkered lilies, pure white bells are included. They are chaste beauties, especially when combined with pristine white daffodils and snowflakes (see page 23).

Bleeding heart is another unique character in the spring garden. Its long arching stems drip with small pink or white hearts. Although it is an easy-to-grow woodland plant, you need to give some consideration to where you place it. Like Virginia bluebells, the foliage of bleeding heart dies back after flowering. Both plants can be planted among hosta, which will emerge as the bluebells and bleeding hearts exit. In a vase, the arms of bleeding heart should extend out farther than the other flowers so they can be seen. This is easy to do since their stems are strong enough to poke into floral foam, and they can be easily positioned.

THE BIGGER GUYS

Flowering trees and shrubs are at their best in spring and join the bulbs blooming along my woodland walk, while my perennial flower borders and cutting garden are only showing green. The blooms on long branches are ideal for overblown arrangements but problematic for the dinner table. I can't explain why it took me a while to realize that the reason the small flowers bloom so far apart on tree and shrub branches is to give floral arrangers the ability to cut them to fit any size arrangement!

One of my favorite things (actually I have two) is a centerpiece from VivaTerra (the "eco" home and garden catalog). It is a low metal tray with upright twisting metal "twigs" that serve as supports for the flower stems you place among them. I was given silver and bronze versions and I use both regularly. The tray holds water a couple of inches deep. I hide the stem bottoms with reindeer moss. Star magnolia is breathtaking when seen this way. The subtly scented flowers last a few days at most, but their twinkle—no matter how brief—is exquisite. Too bad a late, hard frost

OPPOSITE: Forsythia and daffodils are compatible in an umbrella stand on the front porch. BELOW: Star magnolia branches are held up in the twig flower centerpiece from VivaTerra.

or heavy rains can tatter and tear star magnolia's blooms, and too much heat can shatter them in the garden or in the house. But if winter ends gently, the sight of the stars layered throughout the tree will make you stop and gasp. The sight is truly sublime, because the 3- to 4-inch blossoms burst open before the tree leafs out.

Forsythia and dogwood are both excellent for cutting and can last a couple of weeks if they are in a room that's cool or if they are displayed outdoors. In a deep vase, I arrange the taller branches of the shrubs first, crossing them underwater to form a grid to prop up shorter flowers. I like to keep an arrangement of forsythia and daffodils on the front porch to greet everyone from the mailman to dinner guests. It is unexpected and wel-

coming. The daffodils depart after a week, but the
forsythia lasts a few weeks longer because of the
cool nights and the shade of the porch. Indoors in a
warm room, you can expect forsythia to last a week
to 10 days, tops.

Kousa dogwoods (*Cornus kousa*) have an elegant,
refined beauty, especially when covered in constella-
tions of their white star-shaped flowers. The long-
lasting flowers are very useful for flower arrangers.
Each dogwood bloom grows on its own short stem
off the main branch, making it easy to poke into
foam. When a branch is cut into small 4-inch bites,
the starry blooms quickly cover floral foam wreaths,
garlands, or candle cups (devices that hold small
scoops of floral foam on top of candlesticks). I admit
I have quickly assembled a wreath without condition-
ing the Kousa branches first, and the blossoms lasted 5 days or more without a
fuss. Please don't tell that I don't always follow my own advice!

Pink dogwoods (*C. florida rubra*) glow like neon lights in the garden when they
first open. They attract so much attention that they are a wake-up call for spring's
beauty. In flower arrangements, pink dogwoods add a nice punch of color. Yet,
when I combined them in a wreath of screeching pink azalea, they looked calm
and serene. It's all a matter of degree.

When shown in vases, the long stems of dogwood branches can act as a background for cradling giant tree peony flowers (see page 35).

Azaleas and rhododendrons can be used the same way in floral foam or vases. A
branch in water easily supports both the flower and the foliage. In floral foam,

newly opened azalea and rhododendron flowers last 5 days, but the foliage will stay fresh longer. Because of the density of the flowers and foliage, they quickly cover a floral foam wreath and only need a few other flowers, such as pink dogwood blooms, for accents. I have also arranged azaleas in candle cups. Anything, in fact, that holds floral foam can support an azalea in an arrangement. (See Part 2 for more details on candle cups.)

There are so many excellent species and cultivars of rhodies and azaleas available that I won't bore you with the names of the ones I grow. (By the way, both azaleas and rhododendrons share the same Latin family name of *Rhododendron*. It can be confusing.) Choose your favorite colors from a trusted nursery and you can't go wrong. Because of my fondness for roses, I have taken a liking to the rosebud azaleas. Their blooms do look like rosebuds. I particularly like combining them with the single red peony 'America' in a tall vase (see page 1).

TREE PEONIES: GIANTS AMONG US

It is an exaggeration to call tree peonies "trees." They are small shrubs that grow slowly to 4 feet wide and perhaps 6 feet high. But it is no exaggeration to call their blooms giants. They are salad plate size, from 6 to 12 inches across, in white, pink, orange, lavender, or red. They do look good enough to eat but they have a bitter taste from phenol compounds in both foliage and flowers that protect them from deer and rabbits. One flower is a bouquet in itself and, if picked as it opens, will last more than a week in water. My 20-year-old shrub can be counted on for 15 flowers—at least—each spring. The first flowers open near the bottom of the shrub where they are hard to notice, so I always snip them to use as decorations. Atop a present (see page 83) or mixed in with a bunch of dogwood branches, tree peonies certainly garner all the attention. If the flowers are left on the shrub, the seed heads form beautiful, honey-colored stars that are decorative in the winter garden and in holiday wreaths.

OPPOSITE: A bouquet of pink, blue, purple, and white lilacs. BELOW: A nosegay of lily-of-the-valley decorates one gift and a single tree peony flower another.

BLOOMING BUDDIES: LILACS AND PEONIES

Lilacs have a traveling scent that's strong, yet never overpowering. The common lilac is the strongest-scented species, blooming in mid- to late April for about 16 to 20 days. I came to the conclusion years ago that I could never have enough lilacs, so I planted an assortment in different colors, from pink and white to blue and purple. To make a sensational bouquet, all

you need to do is cut a few stems from each color and group them together. (Splitting their ends with a sharp knife or pruners helps them take up water.)

As soon as I saw the lilac cultivar 'Sensation' in a friend's garden, I added it to my own. This unusual lilac is a great beauty, with its purple petals outlined in white and its intoxicating perfume. Its individuality is lost on the bush but makes a big splash in a vase. Combined with the almost-black tulip 'Queen of Night', it is a pairing to be admired.

Every few years an early warm spell pushes the first peonies into bloom so that their flowering overlaps with the common lilacs. It is worth waiting for (but can't be counted on). As the classic lilacs wane, Preston lilacs (*Syringa* x *prestoniae*) open their blooms to extend the lilac season for another few weeks into June. It would be hard to find a more congenial twosome than late-blooming lilacs and early-blooming peonies. They are compatible in color, fragrance, and form in both the garden and the vase. If their beauty doesn't hold your attention, their perfume will. They bring out the best in each other.

OPPOSITE: Pink tree peonies slipped in among pink dogwood branches. BELOW: Preston lilacs, lupine, poppies, and roses are lined up in a glass tube holder.

Preston lilac flowers differ slightly from classic lilacs; Prestons have longer, narrower tubular florets that hang in plumes rather than in larger flared sprays. Their scent, like most late bloomers, is spicy, like Rhone wine. They prolong the lilac season, letting us down slowly. And their long bloom means they can host mid- and late-blooming peonies as well. Popular cultivars include 'James Macfarlane', 'Donald Wyman', and 'Miss Canada'.

Peonies have many different looks. Each peony is a scene-stealer in its own right, and many have a memorable perfume as well. Breeders classify three distinct scents—honey, rose, and an unpleasant odor reminiscent of bitter medicine. The medicinal scent is not a traveling one; keep your nose out of the blooms and you'll never notice it. It's usually a characteristic of the pollen-bearing cultivars. Single red peonies are among the worst offenders for the medicinal scent. However, there are exceptions—'America', a favorite for long bloom and glorious flowers, boasts a lightly sweet breath. Large red chalices of 'America' slipped into a tall vase among rosebud azalea branches is a gorgeous combination and not easily forgotten (see page 1).

Fully double peonies generally have the strongest and sweetest scent. A clump of 'Festiva Maxima', an antique beauty bred in 1851, blooms with blousy bowls of double white flowers splashed with flecks of red, making it easily identifiable. This early bloomer's scent reminds some people of old roses and others of sweet talcum powder. Peonies lavish their fragrance on anyone nearby. If I place a bowl of 'Festiva Maxima' peonies in the entrance, their fragrance wafts up the stairway and scents adjoining rooms. Mixed in an arrangement of assorted peonies and early pink roses in my wicker plant stand on the porch (see front cover), they are unexpected and command attention. No one walks by them without noticing.

A Splash in a Birdbath

To make a big splash at a garden party, I fill a birdbath with flowers. Birdbaths come with their own pedestal, placing the flowers in the spotlight. If I'm in a hurry, I simply float flat or cupped flowers, like large-flowered clematis, hollyhocks, roses, and lilies. For evening, I float candles or set a hurricane glass with a pillar candle in the center. (Hurricanes shield candles from the wind.) For a more extravagant display, I tape blocks of floral foam securely into the bowl of the birdbath to support a large bouquet of flowers. If the birdbath is lightweight and easily moved, it can be placed on a terrace, in a garden, or at an entrance where it is the center of attention. Birdbath arrangements are a perfect display for a garden wedding.

Opposite: A bouquet of daffodils, Virginia bluebells, checkered lilies, and snowflakes sits on top of a birdbath. Below: A rubber boot holds branches of flowering shrubs in a water glass hidden in the boot.

Many other garden staples—wheelbarrows, plant stands, footed urns, terra-cotta pots, hanging baskets, watering cans, bushel baskets, and rubber boots—can all be drafted into use to hold bouquets with spectacular effects. One rainy spring, I slipped tall plastic glasses inside a pair of red boots to outfit them for holding branches of flowering trees. They symbolized the season and made the walk through my woodland garden more entertaining. So use your imagination: Examine all your standbys with an eye to bedecking them with flowers—and have some fun!

GARDEN TIPS FOR SPRING

- One of the reasons my shrub rose bushes have so many blooms is that I don't prune them at all their first few years, except to remove any dead stems. Once the roses have grown into large shrubs, I reduce them by a half or a third in April. The larger the bush, the more roses that bloom.

- There are assorted viburnums, azaleas, and rhododendrons that appear with mid-season and late varieties of bulbs, such as tulips, daffodils, and bluebells. Pair them in both the garden and the vase.

- *Daphne caucasica*, the longest-blooming shrub I know, usually begins its act along with the mid-season bulbs, then meets up with latecomers before continuing long into fall.

- For a long-blooming spring garden, utilize the space around most any tree by naturalizing spring bulbs in irregular drifts out to the extent of the tree's branches.

- One secret to longer-lived hybrid tulips is planting them deeper than recommended. Deeper planting discourages animals from digging up the bulbs for dessert.

- Planting common spring bulbs is as close to a sure thing as a gardener ever gets. The cheaper the bulb, the more likely it will return.

- The quickest way from rags to riches is to plant more bulbs! They take up so little room underground in the garden, reliably return each year with little care from the gardener, and disappear before the summer perennials appear and the annuals are planted.

- Early spring bulbs may be small and meek, but their ability to roll with the punches is miraculous. Never hesitate to add other plants to a bed of early bulbs out of fear of damaging the bulbs.

- The biggest complaints about lilacs are their ungainly growth and bare bottoms. Lilacs need to be kept in their place. Rejuvenation pruning, or removing a third of the branches thicker than 1½ inches in diameter every 5 years, keeps the shrubs below 6 feet tall. An unkempt shrub that hasn't been pruned for decades can be taken down to 6 inches. It will begin again, blooming in about 2 years. Planting peonies at a lilac's feet hides their poorly clad legs.

- Planting in pairs is a simple way to come up with a pleasing design. Pairing a flowering shrub or tree with a cluster of bulbs or perennials that bloom at the same time accomplishes this quite well, and if they combine well in the garden, they often combine well in the vase.

- Peonies are perfectly content no matter if they are ever divided or not. They know their place in the garden and remain there without squawking.

- Don't despair if you don't have room for a lilac-and-peony path. One lilac paired with a few peonies can anchor a flower bed, be a focal point in a front or back lawn, accent a curve in a driveway, or stand at attention next to a garage. For small spaces, try a dwarf lilac, such as 'Miss Kim' with lavender flowers; and 'Palibin', a dark pink bloomer.

A bouquet of red peonies sits on a table under an ornamental cherry tree.

A twig basket filled with floral foam holds an arrangement of roses, columbine, and love-in-a-mist, with ivy trailing out.

SUMMER'S PROFUSION

Summer is a magical time in a garden. It's as close to paradise as you get while keeping your feet on the ground. Everywhere you look, your gaze is returned by flowers. In June if you visit our garden, you'll see it at its peak. Lush perennials and roses camouflage the weeds. Oh, the weeds do make their presence known as the summer progresses, but it doesn't matter because all eyes are on the flowers. To make the most of nature's abundance, we eat and entertain in the garden whenever the weather allows. Even if we are dining next to a flower border, blooms are on our table.

SUMMER FAVORITES AT A GLANCE

Summer is a luxurious season with so many flowers in bloom that bouquets practically make themselves. Many of the perennial flowers listed–balloon flower, Shasta daisies, black-eyed Susans–bloom for months on end. When you add to this the hydrangeas that hold their flowers all summer and into fall, and the annuals that bloom continuously if they are regularly picked, you begin to understand summer's bounty. Plant the prolific bloomers as your staples, then supplement with anything that catches your eye and you'll reap the rewards.

FLOWERS

Agapanthus (*Agapanthus* 'Midnight Blue')

Ageratum (*Ageratum houstonianum*)

Allium (*Allium* sp.)

Astilbe (*Astilbe* sp.)

Balloon flower (*Platycodon grandiflorus*)

Bellflower (*Campanula* sp.)

Black-eyed Susan (*Rudbeckia hirta*)

Butterfly bush (*Buddleja davidii* sp.)

Chaste tree (*Vitex agnus-castus*)

Clematis (*Clematis* sp.)

Coneflower, purple (*Echinacea purpurea*)

Daisies, Shasta (*Chrysanthemum* x *superbum*)

Deutzia (*Deutzia scabra*)

Foxglove (*Digitalis grandiflora*)

Heliotrope (*Heliotropium arborescens*)

Honeysuckle (*Lonicera* sp.)

Hosta (*Hosta* 'Royal Standard')

Hydrangea (*Hydrangea* sp.)

Lady's mantle (*Alchemilla mollis*)

Lily (*Lilium* sp.)

Love-in-a-mist (*Nigella damascena* 'Miss Jekyll Hybrids')

Love-in-a-puff (*Cardiospermum halicacabum*)

Lupine, wild (*Lupinus perennis*)

Money plant (*Lunaria annua*)

Montbretia (*Crocosmia* sp.)

Nicotiana (*Nicotiana* sp.)

Onion, fool's (*Triteleia laxa* 'Queen Fabiola')

Orange, mock (*Philadelphus coronarius*)

Peas, sweet (annual) (*Lathyrus odoratus*)

Peas, sweet (perennial) (*Lathyrus latifolius*)

Phlox, garden (*Phlox paniculata*)

Queen Anne's lace (*Anthriscus sylvestris*)

Roses (*Rosa* sp.)

Snowbell tree, Japanese (*Styrax japonicus*)

Sunflowers (*Helianthus* sp.)

Sweet William (*Dianthus barbatus*)

Thistle, globe (*Echinops ritro*)

Tickseed (*Coreopsis grandiflora*)

Zinnia (*Zinnia* sp.)

FOLIAGE

Dogwood, kousa (*Cornus kousa*) 'Gold Star'

Hosta (*Hosta* sp.)

Ivy (*Hedera* sp.)

BERRIES AND SEED HEADS

Daffodil (*Narcissus* sp.)

Hyacinth, grape (*Muscari* sp.)

The clashing blooms of orange, red, pink, and yellow roses are mixed with the calming green of lady's mantle, blue lupine, and yellow foxgloves. A few red peonies and yellow and orange honeysuckle join the mix.

ROSY FUTURES

To state the obvious, I'm smitten with garden roses. They differ significantly from florist flowers. Garden roses run the gamut from seven-petaled country lasses, to the refined uptight hybrid teas with 20 to 40 petals (the society ladies of the garden), and on to the cabbage roses, buxom beauties each with more than a hundred petals.

OPPOSITE: Roses cavort with sweet William and blue lupine in a glass vase. BELOW: A mock topiary completely covered in roses.

Depending on the cultivar, roses smell sweet, fruity, spicy, or even like a freshly brewed cup of tea. Their perfumes are a mix of fragrances. Many a rose scent is so evasive and unique that it is impossible to capture it in words; catalogs often simply list the scent of roses as sweet. If you are not familiar with the old rose perfume, you have no choice but to plant one of these roses. There is no other way to understand the power of its scent or to understand how it smells.

Sometimes when I deadhead wilted roses to encourage re-bloom, I remove the outer petals and collect the fresh petals at the center. Imitating the Romans, I strew these perfumed petals down a dinner table in wanton

excess, like those at a Roman orgy. Fresh petals hold their scent and last for several days. 'Mr. Lincoln', a red hybrid tea, is the only rose I know that holds its old rose scent when the petals are dried.

It is a paradox that florists charge more for long-stemmed roses even though the cheaper ones on shorter stems last considerably longer. Personally, I think roses on stilts distract from the blossoms' beauty. Unless I am making a giant display for the entrance of my home, when I'm mixing long-stemmed roses with other long-limbed beauties, my roses are on a shorter stem. Unfortunately, though, the more petals a rose has, the shorter its vase life. Yet, I'll first pick the overstuffed blossoms on short stems every time. Roses shed their petals with romantic abandon—what a wonderful way to go!

Along with June's plethora of roses come so many design choices. Do I cut a single stem or fill a bowl to busting with blooms? Should I set up a series of multiples, in short mint julep cups or perhaps tall thin vases, and align them along a mantel or down the middle of a table? Or do I take some time and create mock topiaries, which are conversation starters at a dinner party? Of course, gathering a handful of roses in a glass vase is a sure thing; ditto a floral foam wreath embroidered with roses. I usually hang one on the garden gate.

Occasionally, I try eccentric combinations. Grape hyacinth pods nestled into a bouquet of roses bring both into sharp relief.

When the tiny but prolific buds of our vintage climbing 'Cécile Brunner' bloom, I place one at each place setting tucked into a napkin and then I cluster petite vases of the roses around the table as party favors. Each perfectly formed miniature rose is a wonder rarely seen up close and it's sweetly scented to boot. They were the original sweetheart rose worn by men as boutonnieres a century ago. Today, they are a conversation starter.

Crazy for Chartreuse

I'm fascinated with chartreuse flowers. It is an arresting color—a floral glue to hold diverse tones together, a peacemaker, and a charmer all rolled into one. No matter where I place chartreuse accents, they enhance their cohorts and direct all the attention their way. Even alone, a vase filled with lime-green flowers is unique, unexpected, and sophisticated, but chartreuse is oh-so-much-better in mixed company.

Lady's mantle tops the list and starts the season off. The frothy flower sprays contrast in shape and color with clusters of roses. Lady's mantle can be poked into floral foam and adds a lightness to arrangements. Zinnia 'Envy', *Nicotiana langsdorffii*, and *N. alata* 'Lime Green' are annual, long-blooming chartreuse flowers. All three are so productive that with just half a dozen plants of each, I can cut them weekly. Mixed with blue, they always cause a stir; interspersed with white, they look cool and modern.

OPPOSITE: **Lady's mantle blooms and 'Scarlet Meidiland' roses in a glass vase.** LEFT: A wreath of lady's mantle and columbine decorate a floral foam wreath around the neck of a metal rabbit.

HANGING IT UP

To add a festive atmosphere to a party, I display cut flowers on walls, gates, doors, and trees, placing their beauty, unexpectedly, at eye level. I'm always seeking out interesting flat-backed ceramic or glass "pockets" with rounded fronts to place smack up against a wall. A blue and white one hangs on the back porch wall, always ready for flowers. Sometimes I repeat the blue and white theme with dark blue flowers of heliotrope, purple chaste tree, and white Queen Anne's lace. The vanilla perfume of the heliotrope wafts across the space, inviting guests to linger.

I also use ordinary hanging planters, in anything from metal to straw to terra-cotta, to suspend flowers freely in open spaces or even from the limb of a tree. I hang a garden chandelier from a tree branch over a round table for outdoor dining. The chandelier has a glass vase in the center for a bouquet of flowers and votive candles on outstretched arms. Flowers displayed this way are memorable; their beauty, so ephemeral and delicate, won't be overlooked. The same goes for a simple basket attached to a door, fence, or garden gate. Somehow seeing a bouquet this way makes you look twice, and it is doubly appreciated.

OPPOSITE: Roses, including 'Mary Rose' and 'Veilchenblau', combine with lady's mantle and lupine.
LEFT: A hanging basket holds lilies, coneflowers, agapanthus, balloon flower, and bellflower.

PERENNIAL FAVORITES

Blue flowers are a personal passion. Like chartreuse, they've never met a color they didn't get along with! The spiky blue balls of globe thistle contrast beautifully with the soft petals of most flowers. They are standouts. A mature plant can be counted on for seven stems. You do the math to see how many you need to assure some for the garden and some for cutting. If picked and hung upside down to dry, they can be saved for winter decorations.

Another blue standout is balloon flower. Its flowers first appear as puffy buds, like tiny Wedgwood blue balloons, before opening into star-shaped flowers atop 3-foot stems. Each bud is distinct in an arrangement, and the flowers are at home paired with anything. Obviously, they are radiant in a blue and white bouquet with white roses and lilies. Juxtaposed against yellow foxgloves, they are easily noticed. There are also pink and white and double-blue hybrids, but these are not as prolific bloomers, nor as easy to grow. So many other pink and white flowers work better that they haven't a chance at getting a parking spot in my garden.

OPPOSITE: Salvia, alliums, roses, bachelor's buttons, yellow foxglove, 'Roguchi' clematis, peonies, and more arranged in a pottery vase outfitted with floral foam.

And speaking of yellow foxgloves, *Digitalis grandiflora* is a true perennial. It roams my woodland garden, lightening shady corners. Unlike the biannual foxgloves that send up between two and four flower stems, yellow foxglove reliably returns in early summer and blooms off and on into fall. What more could I ask for? In arrangements, its soft yellow bells glow and reflect the light. A few stems at the back of a bowl of pink roses turn a so-so display into something splendid.

Clusters of garden phlox bloom in assorted pinks, purples, and whites and scent the air with a sweet, talcum powder odor. (Interestingly, I know a few male gardeners who describe its perfume as "peppery and pigsty." It is all a matter of taste.) Phlox can go it alone to form a lush bouquet but it is most content mingling with others. I hung a bunch of phlox in a vase on the gate and included two lengths of curvaceous clematis to twine up and around the posts.

DAISIES DO

Happily, as I age I find myself more drawn to the simplicity of daisies. Daisies are joyful, fun-loving, unassuming, and easygoing. I admire their disarming innocence, their humility, and their ability to rise up again after a storm. The sight of them conjures up sunlit memories of my childhood days and the lazy mornings I spent collecting them from the meadow across the street. And, like all young girls, I passed many an hour plucking off petals one by one to find out whether someone loved me or loved me not. "Daisies do," as Shakespeare wrote, "paint the meadows with delight," and when collected into bouquets they bring that cheerfulness indoors.

There are dozens of flowers with "daisy" as part of their common names and even more with daisylike flowers. They all have petals, known as rays, surrounding a colorful center, or eye. Daisies with white petals and a yellow eye are the most

OPPOSITE: Shasta daisies, coreopsis, and hosta 'Royal Standard' flowers stand in a glass of water in a hollow log. BELOW: A wreath repeats the daisylike shape with different flowers, including chamomile and Shasta daisies, to make it more interesting.

common ones available. Hybridizers have created daisies that are annuals, biennials, or perennials in all the hues of the rainbow, even blue. But they've christened the ox-eye or Shasta daisy as *the* daisy. Wherever Shastas are grown, they are loved for their sparkling white rays, their golden centers, and the delicate droop of their petals. Daisies make wonderful, long-lasting cut flowers. Gathering handfuls to bring indoors is such a nice diversion. No matter which flowers I mix them with or where I place them, they add to the warmth and pleasure of my home.

Another of the most commonly grown daisies is the black-eyed Susan. It blooms for 3 months or more in the garden and lasts 2 weeks in the vase. Using them in an airy bouquet accentuates their independence. They are at home in my wooden bucket with golden Hakone grass. The

beginnings of a wasp's nest clinging to a bare branch that I found late one spring completes the picture.

Purple coneflowers aren't called coneflowers for nothing. Their orange-brown centers point upward, reminding me of the shuttlecocks in a badminton game. These babies look like they're about to take off from a launching pad; with their petals curved back they look like rockets. They lend motion and energy to any display, and that's all the more reason to add them to arrangements. New cultivars come in a gamut of shades, from sunset tones to white, and doubles are also available. The white coneflowers are elegant; I mix them with white lilies and blue agapanthus and balloon flowers in more formal arrangements (see page 50). But the other varieties in loud colors should stay true to their cottage garden beginnings: I prefer them in casual arrangements, such as bunched in an ironstone pitcher or paired with other wildflowers.

Sunflowers resemble daisies on steroids. They come in many different sizes and even a few different colors. They have the sunniest personality. I dare you to look one in the eye without smiling. That alone is the perfect reason to plant some. I poke seeds into the ground in late April, several weeks before the last frost, and I have an assortment to cut for arrangements from July on. Often, I mix sunflowers with black-eyed Susans, their mini-me's. Sometimes I add goldenrod to see if anyone notices. Its bad-boy reputation is undeserved, because its heavy pollen falls to the ground and does not become airborne, so it can't cause allergies.

I gathered a big bunch of sunflowers, conditioned them (see "Guidelines for Conditioning Flowers" on page 195), and took them along on our vacation to the Adirondacks. Their 8-hour car ride out of water didn't faze them. Once we arrived, they made themselves at home in a wooden barrel with hobble bush (*Viburnum lantanoides*) and goldenrod.

OPPOSITE: A wooden barrel becomes a vase for sunflowers, black-eyed Susans, goldenrod, and hobble bush. BELOW: A wooden bucket of black-eyed Susans and Hakone grass is decorated with paper butterflies and a wasp's nest.

ANNUAL DILEMMA

Change is what keeps a garden lively. Yearly additions of annuals always round out my vegetable plot, cutting garden, and flower borders. I experiment with new cultivars and welcome back my old favorites, including ageratum, cosmos, cleome, dianthus, snapdragons, poppies, sweet William, nicotiana, love-in-a-mist, heliotrope, and zinnias. Consequently, my creative urges are challenged and satisfied anew each summer. And since annuals bloom long into fall, they're sensible plants for the busy gardener as well as the intrepid floral designer. I must warn you, however, that it is impossible to choose among all the annuals and only plant a few of them.

My vegetable garden is probably the place where I plant the most annuals. The reseeders are allowed to wander where they may, even in the pathways. Sweet William, an old-fashioned cottage flower, is a biennial that appears early in the season with globes of tiny flowers wafting a baby powder scent. I cut between 4 and 10 stems per plant, although I'm careful to leave numerous blooms to drop seed, assuring next year's crop. If the flowers are cut off early, the plant often returns the next year. Hardy to Zone 4, sweet William has been in gardens since at least the 12th century, so he certainly can care for himself.

Cosmos and cleome (or spider flower) both return unaided year after year from seeds they dropped the year before. They are such benevolent bloomers that I can gather handfuls of posies from just a few plants. In fact, cutting cosmos speeds up the production of flowers and causes the stems to branch. If I snip flowers when they first open and before pollen has formed, I can expect a long vase life of 5 to 7 days. The oddball cosmos 'Sea Shells' has fluted petals in pink, burgundy, or white that scroll out from a gold button center, like a pinwheel. To make sure that 'Sea Shells' visits my garden each summer, I sprinkle seed each year in spring after danger of frost has passed. The cosmos bloom in 2 months.

OPPOSITE: **A wooden bucket holds domes of red, pink, and white sweet William, 'Ballerina' and 'Belinda' roses, white alliums, purple baptisia, and blue forget-me-nots. Iris leaves are folded over and tucked in to form a ruffle.**

The spider flower *Cleome hassleriana* gives cosmos a run for the money because of its speedy growth. Sprouting outward from 5-foot-tall stems, these frenetic spheres exude a pungent lemony scent and usually last for a week after cutting. On bright sunny days the petals curl up but open again as evening approaches. Even curled, the flowers are showy. When cutting, hold the plant's main stem to avoid the thorns that grow where the flowering branch joins it. You will also notice that touching the foliage leaves a sticky residue on your hands, but that's easily washed off. The sticky foliage and the cruel thorns give some gardeners pause. Not me! Cleome's unique blooms are welcome bunched in a pitcher on my kitchen table. They are simply no trouble in the garden, reseeding and returning on their own as far north as Zone 5. Any unwanted seedling can be given to friends or moved to another spot.

OPPOSITE: A child's sand bucket holds an assortment of zinnias, garlic chive flowers, roses, and red salvia.

Love-in-a-mist (see page 192) quickly blooms from seed in 2 months. After flowering, with no help from the gardener, it spreads seed and blankets the earth with blooms, sometimes two or three times before the season wanes. The seedpods are puffs the size of Tootsie Pops, marked with reddish brown spots. They can be collected for winter arrangements and for next year's seeds. But it is the flowers I adore. The fuzzy blue blossoms on foot-high stems look scintillating when combined with roses. Opposites do attract!

Zinnia petals revolve in pinwheels or ruffles in singles or doubles in a wide assortment of colors. I've had freshly cut zinnias last for 2 weeks in bouquets—long after all the other flowers have faded. Zinnias are a symbol of summer, whether bundled together as a single-flower arrangement or partnered with dahlias and sunflowers. And nothing is simpler to grow from seed sown directly in the garden. The seed packet choices are numerous, and the seeds cost just a fraction of the price of a single plant. Blooms often show as early as 6 weeks, and by 8 to 10 weeks, the plants are often frolicking along, inviting all who pass to pick a few flowers.

BULBS AND CORMS

The floriferous bulbs of summer offer flowers made for picking—think fool's onion, alliums (ornamental onions), crinum lilies (in the Amaryllis family), lilies, and Montbretia.

The first of the summer bulbs to bloom is fool's onion. It resembles a galaxy of falling stars. Between 12 and 20 of the 2-inch-long trumpets circle the top of the 2- to 3-foot stems. When I plant fool's onion, I poke the small bulbs a finger length into the soil at the front of the border among my low growers, such as lady's mantle. Fool's onion takes up very little underground room and blooms together with the lady's mantle; the chartreuse clusters of lady's mantle topped by fool's onion's taller blue trumpets are a winning combination. The flowers cheerfully last for 2 weeks in a vase and longer in the garden. The fool is the gardener who doesn't bother to plant it!

OPPOSITE: **Fool's onion in blue water bottles.** BELOW: **Stems of fool's onion, astilbe, and lacecap hydrangea are poked in a glass vase filled with marbles. The marbles hold the stems in place.**

Next the true onions, members of the Allium family, arrive in the garden. They are reputed to repel vampires, and I can testify that they work like a charm: I haven't been bothered for years. The Allium family is best known for its edible members—chives, onions, and leeks—but it includes spectacular ornamentals with floral heads from 2 to 10 inches across. Each carries an onion scent in its bulbs and foliage, but the odor disappears once the stem is put in water. *Allium aflatunense* 'Purple Sensation', with purple balls on 3-foot spires, is the most useful for a garden bouquet. The sturdy stems easily stand tall and proud when braced by floral foam, a floral frog, or even stones. Place a few stems in a glass cylinder vase with glass marbles at the bottom to

create a striking sight. For winter decorations, I save dried blooms that I've plucked straight from the garden after they've browned. This allium's quirky sibling is *A. sphaerocephalon*, the drumstick allium. Each flower head is oval rather than round and crammed with 50 to 100 reddish purple blossoms. That's a sight worth cultivating. Even before their green flower buds color up and open in late June or July, they look decorative in a vase. Alliums are perfectly placed in the garden when they lead the eye through the border with eye-catching clumps, randomly hip-hopping along.

The majestic crinum lilies bloom about the same time as common lilies, yet are better known in Southern gardens because many of them can't take cold. *Crinum* x *powellii* is an exception, hardy all the way to Connecticut (Zone 6). Its 3-foot stems are topped with 8 to 10 white or pink lilylike flowers with the scent of violets, a fragrance that will make you swoon. The plant x *Amarcrinum* is a cross between a crinum and an amaryllis. They are elegant flowers, particularly beautiful sans partners, arranged simply in a pitcher or fluted vase where their fragrance and beauty can't be missed.

Oriental and Chinese trumpet lilies also are known for their sweet breath. One of these powerfully perfumed lilies can scent a garden, while a clump of them can send a fragrant greeting over a hedge or wall, around the corner, and often far down the block and into open windows. When lilies are in bloom, all other fragrances pale; their perfume catches the passerby and makes him look back to admire the flower's beauty. No man-made perfume ever smelled so good.

OPPOSITE: Shasta
daises, Montbretia, and
lilies in a glass vase.
ABOVE: 'Golden
Splendor' lilies,
foxgloves, Shasta
daisies, tiger lilies,
hydrangeas, globe
thistle, Queen Anne's
lace, and more in an
orange vase. ABOVE
RIGHT: Ageratum,
coneflowers, phlox,
roses, sweet peas,
crape myrtle, and x
Amarcrinum in a
Chinese bucket.

I prefer lilies with large outwardly facing trumpets, rather than ones that look upward as the scentless Asiatic lilies do. Turkscap lilies, *Lilium martagon,* are my favorites, too. They face down with their petals curving up like flaps on a winter hat. They are all personality and perfume. As a consequence of being pollinated at night, they are strongly perfumed after dark.

'Golden Splendor' is a Chinese trumpet, true to its name. It stands 4 feet or more above the annual garden at our swimming pool. It's never been disturbed by my yearly planting around it, nor has it ever needed staking. Chinese trumpets can be counted on to return for more years than the Oriental lilies. Mine are closing in on

two decades. They look so good in the garden, I used to hesitate to pick them. Consequently, I planted a group in the vegetable garden where I snip with impunity.

In an all-white arrangement of feathery astilbe plumes and fluffy astrantia buttons, the smooth petals of 'Casa Blanca' lily sparkle, and its heavenly perfume makes the simple bouquet something quite extraordinary. But be advised when picking lilies for arrangements: Cut as little of the stem as needed. The lily depends on its leaves and stems to

ABOVE: A wicker plant stand filled with floral foam holds a bouquet of lilies, astilbe, astrantia, and balloon flowers.

nurture its bulb while it forms next year's flower. Be aware, too, that the pollen of lilies is easily rubbed or shaken off the flowers and may stain clothing, hands, and noses poking in for a whiff. Florists regularly clip off the stamens to prevent such problems. But I like their bright yellow nobs, dangling on an angle, as if they might lose their grip at any moment. They are the beauty marks on the face of a lily, and I usually don't clip them off. At times I've been caught like a clown with a yellow nose, but I reason that there are worse things I could do.

Montbretia (*Crocosmia* x *crocosmiiflora*) is a late summer bloomer with spikes of star-shaped flowers in hot colors ranging from yellow to orange to scarlet. In the garden, their slim hips slip easily between other summer bloomers. Every 3 or 4 years, they can be divided and replanted in new areas to continue expanding their families. These genuinely selfless bloomers are never troublesome. Red montbretia's slinky 3-foot stature combines well with Shasta daisy's rounder one. Each accentuates the other. The result is more sophisticated than either flower going solo.

WOODLAND TREASURES

When hiking with friends on our property in New York's Adirondack Mountains, I wear a backpack to carry home the treasures we find in the field and on the forest floor. In our meadow, black-eyed Susans, goldenrod, asters, ironweed, and Joe Pye weed wave in the breeze. They are so plentiful that clipping a few here and there is never noticed.

In the shady woods, we collect pigskin puffballs, brightly colored mushrooms, moss, fungus, lichen, berries, and whatever else catches our eye. Once we return, we look up their names in trail guides to get acquainted as we arrange them in floral foam wreaths. Up close and personal is where we can all begin to understand Mother Nature's wily and wonderful ways. The wreaths we make might not be the most beautiful, but they are the most personal.

RIGHT: A floral foam wreath covered in bunchberries, blueberries, mushrooms, pinecones, bark, and moss.

THE LENGTHS I GO TO

Many vines, including clematis, honeysuckle, and sweet pea, have extremely long-lasting flowers, yet are rarely cut for arrangements. This is a shame. Vines create a sense of spontaneity both in the garden and in bouquets. When using them in arrangements, I poke their stems in water or foam and let them softly curve down in front of a vase or up over the handle of a basket. A long length of a tall grower can garland a table or a porch railing. But even if you only snip the flowers on short stems, vines make beguiling bouquet additions.

OPPOSITE: A bouquet of tulips, iris, lilacs, pink and blue bluebells, variegated vinca, double flowering cherry, and 'Montana' clematis in a basket with a handle to carry to a friend. BELOW: A garland of flowers wound around a rope.

CLEMATIS—THE GARDEN'S SEAMSTRESS

I think of clematis as the garden's seamstress, because these lovely vines loosely stitch plants together with an overlay of flowers as they thread their way up, over, and around anything in their path. As they grow, looping their leaf stems around their host, they add a softening touch to the garden. A clematis vine blooms from

PARTY TIME

What's one to do when presented with a magnum of champagne? How do you chill it? It won't fit in the fridge unless everything else is removed. The only other solution, I realized, is to throw a party and ice it down in a trash can garlanded with flowers.

Bill Barrick, a good friend and house guest, put his doctorate in horticulture to work making the garland. First, Bill draped a rope around the can to measure the length of the garland. He then wired flowers and foliage freshly picked from the garden onto the rope. Balloon flowers, yarrow, daisies, roses, and everything else he picked lasted through the evening and for much of the next day. The garland was finished in about a half hour and was the highlight of the party. It goes to show, no container is too "trashy" to be dressed with flowers.

3 weeks to several months, depending on the cultivar. For sheer size of bloom, clematis 'Vyvyan Pennell' (see page 200) is awarded bragging rights. She is the boldest and broadest clematis in my garden—fully 7 inches across and double when she blooms in early summer on old growth. Her sumptuous velvety purple gown begs to be stroked. There is no walking past her. 'Vyvyan' shouldn't have to share the limelight, so I display one flower floating in a fishbowl on a coffee table. Or, I place one as a focal point in a bouquet. In fall when she re-blooms on new growth, her flowers are slightly smaller and single, yet she still causes me to linger.

Large-flowered clematis abound in a wide selection of colors. 'Henryi' only has to bat his dark eye and I stop to admire his white, starlike face. The pink pinwheels of 'Nelly Moser' are striped with deep carmine. C. 'Jackmanii Rubra' is royal purple, while 'Ernest Markham' is a striking red. I could name a hundred more. Suffice it to say, plant at least a half dozen in your garden for a gorgeous assortment.

OPPOSITE AND ABOVE: Proof that sometimes the container is as important as the flowers within, I nested small posies of clematis 'Roguchi', orange turkscap lilies, and honeysuckle into a reproduction sugar mold. A long, low slab of wood, the mold has half a dozen cylindrical holes fitted with metal. Originally these openings were used to measure raw sugar, but they're perfect for displaying flowers or candles. I put small pieces of floral foam into each opening, then poke in the blossoms.

The sweet autumn clematis (C. terniflora) is an entirely different beauty. This high-stepping vine struts its stuff toward the end of summer, exploding with hundreds of tiny frothy white flowers wafting a sweet vanilla scent. The perfume floats through the garden and can be detected even before I see the flowers. I cut long streamers to garland a table or festoon a chandelier. They perfume the surrounding air for a day or two without water and announce, as everyone knows, there's a party.

Clematis 'Roguchi' is my longest bloomer, from early May through September. The cobalt blue bells ring out for attention. Each flower is attached to the vine on

a 6- to 8-inch stem, so it can be clipped off without shortening the vine or disturb-
ing the garden display. Poked into floral foam, the strong, sturdy stems can be
positioned to ring in any direction. Like most clematis flowers, 'Roguchi' lasts 2
weeks in water but slightly less in foam.

As if a beautiful face were not enough, the seedpods of many clematis are
stunning to behold. *C. orientalis*, an early summer bloomer with nodding yellow bells, is a fine example. Once the blooms stop coming, seed heads of
silken threads spun into golden balls cover the vines in splendor for the rest
of summer. I like the seed heads in arrangements almost as much as the
flowers. The heads tolerate a blast of hair spray in the vase to keep them
looking good for a few weeks. It holds them in place so they don't fly away,
spreading their seed (see page 76).

SWEET PEAS

I cherish sweet peas as both annuals and perennials. Both flower on short sturdy stems off the main shoot and are wonderful mixers, but only the annual carries the perfume of the gods. Though the annuals are troublesome to grow, they're well worth it. They have to be started indoors 2 to 3 months before they can be transplanted outside to bloom in June. In the high heat of summer, they stop blooming and quickly go to seed if I forget for even a day or two to pick off all their dead flowers. The only way to explain their behavior is that they have a basic need

OPPOSITE AND BELOW: A bunch of sweet peas brings unique beauty and heavenly fragrance everywhere—from the dining room table to the garden gate.

to be noticed, and once you turn your attention elsewhere, they sulk. I'm sure you've known people like that. But there is no match for their perfume and delicate beauty that's a translucent wash of color. (I am especially fond of blue sweet peas but I must caution you: If their petals are wet, their blue dye will stain your hands, clothes, and tablecloths.) It's a great luxury to have a whole vase of these annuals; their perfume scents a whole room and beyond.

On the other hand, perennial sweet peas carry the family's good looks and are a cinch to grow, even sprawling along dusty roadsides. I haven't yet found a bouquet that either the annual or the perennial sweet pea (or both) didn't enhance.

HONEYSUCKLE

OPPOSITE: Two long stems of honeysuckle twist together and are pinned around a dessert table. Chaste tree and 'Stargazer' lilies are in a vase. BELOW: Roses and honeysuckle spill out of a candle cup.

Not all honeysuckles are fragrant, but all *Lonicera* are beautiful when covered with clusters of fetchingly shaped flowers. Some are white, others are yellow, purple, pink, or orange, and many are artistically flushed in more than one hue. There are many to recommend. I have the fragrant Hall's honeysuckle (*Lonicera japonica* 'Halliana', which can be invasive) hanging over the entrance to my home and the scentless but splendid *L.* x *heckrottii* 'Goldflame' and *L.* x *brownii* 'Dropmore Scarlet' in my garden. They can be cut to any length to garland a table or drape over the rim of a bowl. I clip a foot or more from the tips of blooming shoots for floral foam arrangements.

LOVE-IN-A-PUFF

The idiosyncrasies of nature are in full play in love-in-a-puff, an annual vine known for its green papery puffs. The 2-inch round seedpods form continuously from midsummer until heavy frost. When the pods ripen to brown, they are meant to be popped. Inside each are three jet-black seeds, each marked with a perfectly shaped, bright white heart—hence the plant's name. The unique pods are eye-catching dangling out of a flower arrangement. The vine's tiny white flowers are not much to look at, but the puffs are unforgettable. This gentle climber is easy to grow, as its wispy limbs gently climb by pulling themselves up by tendrils through shrubs or other vines, where the puffs hang as an added frill (see page ix).

FOCUS ON FOLIAGE

Summer leaves can be scene-stealers in their own right. Variegated dogwood does that every time. When I placed a group of cuttings at the base of a bouquet, it became the lure, stealing glances from the roses.

Ivy boasts foliage that is so long lasting I don't bother to condition it. It outlasts every flower. Clipping ivy regularly and adding it to arrangements keeps it in bounds in the garden.

I grow hostas for their patterned foliage rather than their flowers. The only hosta blossom that interests me is 'Royal Standard'. Its white flowers are often mistaken for lilies when they are seen in a vase, and their rich sweet scent completes the hoax. At summer's end, I used them for a large mock topiary with multiple branches on a table in the gazebo. Melded with fragrant sweet autumn clematis, the mingling perfumes captured anyone who walked in.

The varying sizes and colors of hosta leaves can form an interesting runner down a table (see page 71) or, when placed to radiate out from the center, the leaves become a textured tablecloth. When I make nosegays to take as hostess presents, I wrap their stems with hosta leaves. Another plus: Hosta leaves are slow to rot. This means I can use them underwater to line the inside of a glass vase. Just one large leaf, or a few smaller ones, curved inside the vase instantly changes the look of it, making it far more interesting than bare flower stems. Green naturally highlights any flower you tuck within; dahlias in their crayon colors certainly benefitted (see page 91).

OPPOSITE: 'Gold Star' dogwood, crinum lilies, and clematis and daffodil seed heads in a white vase. ABOVE: A wire funnel holds 'Gold Star' dogwood, roses, sea holly, salvia, and flowering tobacco. ABOVE RIGHT: Hosta leaves form a ruffled tablecloth under a wine holder of sweet peas and echinops.

Occasionally, when I cut hosta leaves, slugs are clinging to them. They get the "two-finger squish," no reprieves. But just in case, rinse every individual leaf off, checking both sides before arranging. Once, in my haste, I missed a couple of the creatures. They appeared at the dinner table floating belly up in the crystal vase, and there were a lot of laughs at my expense. Actually, it was a memorable mistake—I might do it again just for laughs!

Hakone grass (*Hakonechloa macra* 'Aureola') glows like golden tresses in a shady border, the grass parting to one side as if it had just been brushed. At the base of the grass are strong, straight, short stems that can be easily poked into floral foam. They can be positioned to drape in any direction, to capture the look of a meadow-in-a-basket or to mimic tail feathers in a wooden swan (see page 166). I've also wrapped strands on packages and baskets as if they were ribbons (see page 83).

FLOWERING SHRUBS AND TREES

The earliest summer shrub to bloom is mock orange, and boy is it welcome! Scented by the gods, it is a treat to work with, especially when cutting and arranging the stems. Their perfume envelops me, and I am carried away by happy thoughts, both remembrances of things past and dreams of the future. The foliage and the flowers last 5 days or more in floral foam, if the surrounding air is cool. I cut long branches for over-the-top arrangements, but it's more enjoyable to cut small pieces to cover wreaths and garlands. The more I cut, the more I awaken the plant's perfume—and the longer I can bathe in its scent. A floral foam wreath or a garland made from a floral foam form is quickly covered by its dense foliage and double white blooms. A 9-foot length fit perfectly along the back of a bench as a festive decoration for a garden party (see pages 184 to 185). It could just as easily have been for a wedding.

OPPOSITE: A birdbath overflowing with flowers of deutzia, alliums, lupine, peony, dame's rocket, clematis, and wisteria. BELOW: A wooden swan wears plumes of butterfly bush as tail feathers.

The double-flowered fuzzy deutzia also blooms from late spring through early summer. This tall spreading shrub has elegant long arching branches that cascade down like a fountain with clusters of double white bells to ring out in the breeze. There are so many long-lasting flowers that it really begs to be cut for bouquets. I've cut branches to fill the large birdbath on my terrace for parties. After I've taped bricks of floral foam into the

bowl, I arrange the branches so they can be seen from all sides. The tallest branches are in the middle, transitioning gradually to the shortest branches around the edges. Once the shape of the bouquet is set by the deutzia, I add other blue and purple flowers for accents: blue lupine, love-in-a-mist, allium, 'Roguchi' clematis, and nepeta.

Butterfly bush and chaste tree share a similar attraction: The tips of their branches are covered with flowery spires made up of tiny fragrant blossoms. Butterfly bush has a honeyed sweetness and chaste tree has a baby powder scent. Both put on a show for several months. Chaste tree has lilac blue flowers, and butterfly bushes come in an assortment of blues, purples, and pinks with white and yellow cultivars, too. In flower arrangements, they are both welcome (see pages 75 and 78).

OPPOSITE: Hydrangea 'Annabelle' forms a ring around lacecap hydrangeas. BELOW: A birdbath outfitted with floral foam supports a bouquet of lilies nestled among mophead and lacecap hydrangeas.

Giant flowers are my weakness, so I have yet to meet a hydrangea I didn't like. They are in-your-face gorgeous in white, pinks, and blues and last for months both outside on the bush and inside if they are dried. The huge flower heads lend themselves to oversize bouquets, and it's fun to combine the different varieties. Since birdbaths seem made to put flowers in their proper place— on a pedestal—it stands to reason that birdbaths and hydrangeas are a perfect match. Yet, hydrangeas can also be scaled down for smaller purposes. Whether a rounded mophead (*Hydrangea macrophylla*), a conical oakleaf (*H. quercifolia*), or a flat-topped lacecap (*H. macrophylla* 'Lacecap'), all these flower heads consist of many florets that can be easily broken apart. The delicate blossoms are especially winsome in a wreath or a candle cup.

GARDEN TIPS FOR SUMMER

- Roses re-bloom sooner if you nip off faded ones at the top of their neck just below their bloom, rather than deadheading them back to the first five leaves.

- Once-blooming roses do not flower continuously, but they are good investments because they blossom so abundantly. My 15-year-old 'Climbing Cecile Brunner' rose clings to the ivy climbing our house and reaches up to our roof. Even if I pick all the blooms I reach, there are still hundreds dangling overhead.

- Allow a few lady's mantle flowers to go to seed for next year's babies.

- Balloon flowers re-bloom quicker if you deadhead individual blossoms, rather than removing the whole stem.

- Phlox cultivars are notorious for powdery mildew. Through an unconscious 20-year selection process, I have always removed mildewed specimens, and the unblemished ones I've left behind have flourished year after year, filling in the empty spaces.

- Cosmos readily reseed once sown. They faithfully return to my cutting garden—not in the same place and often between rows, but who cares!

- A seed pack of the biennial sweet William planted at the back of my vegetable garden 25 years ago colonized a corner, and its flowers return every year.

- Although fool's onion is a California native, it thrives in Zones 6 to 10. Gardeners in colder Zones 3 to 5 dig them up and replant them yearly as I do with my dahlias and gladiolas.

- If carefully planned, an assortment of clematis cultivars can yield three seasons of continuous bloom—four if you count the decorative golden seedpods that stay through winter. Check bloom times, plan accordingly, and train some choices up the bare legs of roses or honeysuckle to act as stockings.

- Keep an organic garden and forego chemical dependence on fertilizers, pesticides, and fungicides. It is not healthy to handle flowers and foliage doused with poisons. Nature's way—yearly dollops of compost on garden beds—keeps most plants happy, even roses.

- Pinch off spent blossoms of annuals and perennials to prevent the formation of seed. Once they produce seeds, they often stop blooming. Deadheading encourages plants to re-bloom.

- No matter what the size of your garden, lily bulbs are easy to tuck into borders, under shrubs, between perennials, and into pots. I've squeezed in dozens, including favorites 'Star Gazer' and 'Casa Blanca', to grow up through the outer skirts of some roses and a chaste tree, and I couldn't be more pleased. Since lilies grow straight up on single, scantily clad stems, they take up very little room. And the bulbs are deeply planted—usually 6 to 8 inches—so they leave space for other plants above. Luckily, lilies do like to have their ankles shaded by the skirts of other plants, while their heads bloom in the sun.

Flowers topping gifts include rows of daisies attached with double-stick tape; a single peony; a bunch of dried money plant; a nosegay of echinops and ageratum; a hydrangea; a grid of inkberry leaves; and a bouquet holder of assorted flowers (see page 190).

A bouquet in the hand, made of freshly cut dahlias for the house.

FALL'S HORN OF PLENTY

Autumn's burst of glory delights the senses even as it signals the end of the gardening cycle. Although roses, dahlias, hydrangeas, and annuals seamlessly smooth the transition from summer to fall, it's the unsung autumn bloomers that bring the season to its crescendo. Shades of blue and purple dominate the landscape; think hardy ageratum, autumn crocus, monkshood, morning glory, and salvias, just to name a bunch. And then there are the berries, glowing like precious jewels. So many to choose from! Here are my fall favorites. I'm sure that as each fall season comes and goes, I'll unearth a few more.

FALL FAVORITES AT A GLANCE

Fall is known for its blazing foliage colors. As a plus, foliage often lasts for weeks in arrangements. Brightly colored foliage and ornamental berries dominate my fall bouquets. There are so many different sizes, shapes, and colors of leaves and berries that fill my vases I don't even notice there are fewer and fewer flowers coming into bloom as the season wanes. With the long bloom of monkshood, Sheffield mums, and dahlias, I have plenty of flowers to add a focal point, if I am so inclined, to my clusters of foliage. I often keep the same foliage and change the look by adding different flowers each week.

FLOWERS

Ageratum, hardy (*Eupatorium coelestinum*)

Anemone, Japanese (*Anemone hupehensis* var. *japonica, A.* x *hybrida*)

Aster, New England (*Aster novae-angliae* 'Harrington's Pink')

Butterfly bush (*Buddleja* sp.)

Chaste tree (*Vitex agnus-castus*)

Crocus, autumn (*Colchicum* sp.)

Cup and saucer vine (*Cobaea scandens*)

Dahlias (*Dahlia* sp.)

Fuchsia, Cape (*Phygelius capensis* 'Yellow Trumpet')

Goldenrod (*Solidago canadensis*)

Hydrangea (*Hydrangea* sp.)

Joe Pye weed (*Eupatorium purpureum*)

Mandevilla (*Mandevilla splendens*)

Monkshood (*Aconitum* sp.)

Morning glory (*Ipomoea tricolor* 'Heavenly Blue')

Mums, Sheffield (*Chrysanthemum koreanum* 'Sheffield')

Roses (*Rosa* sp.)

Salvias (*Salvia* sp.)

Sunflowers (*Helianthus* sp.)

Verbena (*Verbena bonariensis*)

Zinnias (*Zinnia elegans* sp.)

FOLIAGE

Bamboo, dwarf heavenly (*Nanina domestica* 'Wood's Dwarf')

Burning bush or Winged euonymus (*Euonymus alatus*)

Geraniums, scented (*Pelargonium* sp.)

Grasses, ornamental (*Miscanthus* sp.)

Hydrangea, oakleaf (*Hydrangea quercifolia*)

Maple, Japanese (*Acer palmatum*)

Oak, pin (*Quercus palustris*)

Sweetgum (*Liquidambar styraciflua*)

BERRIES AND SEED HEADS

Beautyberry (*Callicarpa bodinieri* 'Profusion')

Crabapples (*Malus* sp.)

Crape myrtle (*Lagerstroemia indica*)

Euonymus, European (*Euonymus europaeus*)

Firethorn (*Pyracantha coccinea*)

Porcelain berry (*Ampelopsis brevipedunculata*)

Rose hips (*Rosa* sp.)

Viburnum, linden (*Viburnum dilatatum*)

OPPOSITE: Dahlias, smoke bush, mandevilla, and roses use a copper watering can as a vase.

ROSY OUTLOOK

Although roses slow down in the high heat of August, they revive once cool nights are the norm. Indeed, September's roses are almost as plentiful as June's. Many keep coming, albeit more slowly, through October and into November. Surprisingly, once in mid-November, I counted 19 blooms in shades of pink, apricot, and yellow on 'Abraham Darby', a vigorous English rose. On 'Heritage', another English stunner, I cut a dozen pink, large, cup-shaped flowers. And 'Scarlet Meidiland', typically the last shrub rose to close up shop in mid-December, held out half a dozen sprays of small flowers. Oddly enough, those sprays proved the longest-lasting roses in the vase. Other rose bushes had a few blooms, but none decked out like these three varieties. Since I never know if I'll have red rosebuds in December, I collect them earlier and hang them to dry. Then they're ready to use in holiday trimmings.

Unfortunately, at this time of year, the rose bushes themselves are ugly ducklings. Most of their leaves have dropped and the few remaining ones look sad and old. The good news is that I don't have to remove much foliage when arranging, and the flowers look as glorious as ever indoors.

One appeal of roses is that they can be dressed up or down. They are happy anywhere, in any container, mixed with any other plants. Combined with deep blue monkshood, roses look regal, their coral and pink tones appearing deeper and

richer. In a copper watering can filled to over-flowing with dark red roses, dahlias, and branches from a dusky smoke bush *(Cotinus coggygria),* the roses evoke a dreamy, melancholy mood (see page 87). Roses lose their elegant postures and seem much more "down home" combined with fall foliage, berries, and their own "hips." Shocking pink euonymus pods steal the show from the roses with their zany antics: They open as they dry to reveal neon orange seeds.

So the flowers aren't the whole story. As cold weather settles in, many roses expend energy producing rose hips, the fruits and seeds of the shrub. Hips come in all sizes, in teardrops or balls, and in shades of orange, burgundy, or red. They glisten on shrubs, in arrangements, and on wreaths, and quite naturally, they look wonderful combined with roses. However, only the small, hard hips last for months after picking. This group includes once-blooming ramblers—from the invasive roadside menace, *Rosa multiflora,* to genteel ladies like 'Climbing Cecile Brunner', 'Ballerina', 'The Fairy', 'Blush Noisette', and *R. eglanteria.* These are but a few of the hundreds of shrubby roses with petite hips to spare. If the birds don't gobble them up, the hips stay on the bushes throughout winter. The ones I pick are given a quick spray with satin shellac to hold their color and shine. They last indefinitely and are recycled from one arrangement to another all winter long (see pages 126 and 131). The larger cherry-tomato-size hips from *rugosa* roses and other large-flowered bloomers are fleshy and rot after a week or so. Recognizing their limitations, I use them in arrangements with fall foliage and hydrangeas, too. They still last longer than many flowers.

OPPOSITE: European euonymus berries combined with roses. ABOVE: Assorted roses including 'Abraham Darby' and 'Heritage' mix it up with monkshood.

Dahlia Daze

Dahlias are the First Ladies of fall. They may be brassy and outspoken or sweetly shy, but they garner most of the attention. They bloom on strong stems modeling an array of guises; there's no single look. Their petals might explode in spurts of fireworks or mimic the tight precision of a crew cut. Shapes, sizes, and even patterns of individual petals vary. With the exception of clear blue, dahlias come in a full spectrum of shades and many bicolors. The flowers themselves might be miniatures less than an inch across, giants more than a foot wide, or somewhere in between. To reflect their diversity, dahlias are classified into a dozen categories by size and form. The categories include anemone, ball, cactus, collarette, peony, pompon, and waterlily, among others. You get the point—whatever your wish, dahlias deliver.

Any gardener who values cut flowers plants a minimum of a dozen dahlia tubers (fleshy underground stems) in the garden or in pots. Each tuber blooms for 3 months or more, from midsummer to killing frost. Each plant averages 20 flowers, providing a continuous supply for cutting. Most of my dahlias have been with me for a quarter century, although I occasionally add a new face I can't resist.

For sheer drama, I like tubers with plate-size flowers. They bring out the braggart in us all. 'Bodacious' is a sumptuous beauty with bright red petals. When her petals curl up, she flashes yellow lightning and is quite a sight. 'Lavender Ruffles' is tamer, a sweetheart with softly toned petals, reminding me of the ruffles on my prom dress. Although these Amazons are good mixers, they also are mesmerizing alone or in small groups. If I

combine them with others, it is in huge arrangements for my home's entrance or for a tall planter outdoors.

While one or two tubers of the Amazons are enough, it is hard to limit the number of other tubers with 3- to 7-inch flowers, since they come in such unique colors and designs. Dahlias effortlessly mingle with roses, salvia, monkshood, ornamental grasses, hydrangea, berries, Japanese anemone, and morning glories—you name it. Like roses, dahlias move easily from china bowl to wooden bucket, mock topiary to candle cup, glass vase to plant stand.

OPPOSITE: A wreath of dahlias, hydrangeas, and rose hips on a garden ornament. ABOVE: Dahlias in a glass vase with a hosta leaf lining the sides and hiding their stems.

THE PERSONALITIES
OF FLOWERS

Flowers, like people, have personalities. That was one of life's early lessons for me. As a college student, a would-be boyfriend compared me to a daisy, when the elegance and beauty of a rose or the mysterious glamour of the orchid would have been more to my liking. Needless to say, his advances were rebuffed. It was only later in life that I came to realize that good looks, even in flowers, can be a snare. The beauty of a hybrid tea rose takes a gardener great pains to preserve; a daisy cares for itself. A daisy radiates happiness like no other flower: This modest beauty is easygoing and contented, traveling the roadside without a care, dancing in the wind, unfazed by the rain. Daisies love the sun but they also bloom in the shade. They are role models for us all.

Love-in-a-mist, on the other hand, is the crazy hat lady down the street. Lilies are glamorous movie stars, drenched in their own perfume. Sunflowers are every-

OPPOSITE: A wooden bucket filled with floral foam holds dahlias, hydrangeas, burning bush, and pineapple sage. BELOW: Dahlias and monkshood embody the blazing colors of fall.

one's friend, always there to cheer you on, with never a sour note. Dahlias are the church ladies lending a helping hand, fitting in nicely wherever they are needed. Zinnias remind me of soldiers with stiff stems standing at attention. Tulips' softly curving stems are like young beauties bending for their first kiss.

I could go on describing the personalities of other flowers—the sassy turkscap lily, the sophisticated orchid, the country bumpkin black-eyed Sue, the uptight obedience plant, and the funky tiger lily. But I'd rather let you take the time to discover and admire the many charms of flowers and to keep their personalities in mind while arranging them.

HEADY HYDRANGEA

I admire hydrangeas for their resilience. What other plant has flowers that open in early summer and—if I don't cut them for bouquets—stay until I remove them in late March, a full 9 months later? Pelted by rain, twisted in wind, pounded by hail, frozen in ice, and buried in snow, they hang on through winter and usually don't show the wear. How do they do that? Miraculously, the longer hydrangea flowers have been on the bush, the longer they last in water. Once cool weather sets in, and their petals rustle like tissue paper, they hold their color when dried for winter bouquets. The flowers do dry naturally in a vase of water, although their heavy heads bend their stems. If they are gathered together with a rubber band and hung upside down to dry in a dark place for a few weeks, their stems dry straight and their flowers don't fade.

Some hydrangeas change color as they age, making them even more interesting. 'Annabelle', the first hydrangea to bloom, starts the season bright white and ends up chartreuse by summer's end. Oakleaf hydrangeas start the summer white and blush to pink once cool nights are the norm in fall. Go figure!

OPPOSITE: A basket of hydrangea 'Snowflake' on a bench. BELOW: A wreath of mophead hydrangeas works for a garden party when a glass chimney protects the candle from the wind.

BELTING OUT THE BLUES

Monkshood, a perennial classic, adds to the brilliant crayon colors of fall foliage. Its splendid deep blue flowers bloom along the stem, opening at the top first. Gradually more flowers open up, making their way down the stem. But the show doesn't stop there: As the flowers fade, bright lime green seedpods form—a nice contrast with the blue flowers below. (As the pods brown, I clip them off so they don't distract.) To "shake it up" a bit, I like to give the predictable marriage of blue and white a kick with pink dahlias. (Note: When handling monkshood, some gardeners wear gloves because all parts of the plant are poisonous.)

'Heavenly Blue' morning glories are flowers with a perpetual wink. New blooms open each day and close up at night. In the garden, it is impossible to keep them down. They weave through shrubs like a motorcycle in a traffic jam. Recently, I yanked off a long, limber limb that strayed from the arbor, wound up one sunflower, then reached over and clutched several others together into a tight bunch. It was a group hug! But I don't condone public displays of affection in the garden—what would the neighbors think? I tossed the stem on a compost heap and returned a few days later to see it merrily blooming along, the king of the heap; its foliage was as fresh as the day I cut it. Compost never looked so good.

OPPOSITE: Swamp maple leaves mixed in a vase with monkshood. Oak, geranium, and burning bush leaves; crabapples; monkshood and ageratum; and a strawflower decorate the packages. BELOW: Morning glories bloom with dahlias.

It was obvious: 'Heavenly Blue' wanted to be included in my arrangements. So, taking a cue from its wanton nature, I wove a 2-foot stem through a pitcher of orange dahlias and clematis 'Roguchi', letting the tail loop across the vase. The blue saucer-shaped blooms charged the simple handful of flowers with electricity. The arrangement reminded me of an Old Master painting. Artists often added morning glories to their arrangements, letting them drape over the edge of the vase and scamper along the table.

SAGE ADDITIONS

OPPOSITE: A cutting basket holding pink and red roses, pineapple sage, hardy ageratum, and monkshood. **ABOVE:** Assorted fall salvias including Mexican sage combine with monkshood and beautyberry.

My gardening didn't have a sage beginning. Aside from the culinary sages in the salvia genus, I only grew blue salvia, *Salvia farinacea* 'Victoria.' But decades later I bumped into the later bloomers—the gorgeous sage siblings—and discovered I had not been properly introduced to the family. These fall bloomers rejuvenate the tired garden, standing as tall as 3 to 5 feet above it. Salvias run the range from annuals and biennials to both tender and hardy perennials and sub-shrubs. The family resemblance is apparent in their square stems, opposite leaves, and tall, skinny floral spikes. The individual flowers are mostly tubular—some are hooked at the end, and others split like lobster claws or parrot beaks. Most blue and purple salvias easily air dry for winter arrangements, but, strangely, the red, pink, and yellow varieties don't.

The tall fall-blooming sages store rich volatile oils in their foliage and produce an array of aromas from fruity to medicinal. If leaves are broken or brushed against, their heady odor rushes up to engulf me. While most of the shorter annual salvias (such as *S. farinacea* and *S. splendens*) are scentless, pineapple sage (*S. rutilans*, formerly *S. elegans*) and anise-scented sage (*S. guaranitica*) acknowledge their scents in their names. Mexican bush sage (*S. leucantha*) and prairie sage (*S. azurea* subsp. *pitcheri*) are fruity, while 'Purple Majesty' is citrusy. Because of the sages' heady perfume, it is a pleasure to strip off the foliage of stems that will stand below the waterline in my arrangements.

Pineapple sage blooms in September with long arching racemes of candy-apple-red flowers. It is a plant I love as much for its scented leaves as for its flowers. I flavor my iced tea with its leaves and use them like mint, shredded on fruit, to flavor drinks, and to garnish desserts. And this sage is lovely in all kinds of bouquets. For a door ornament in a copper cone, I nestled some stems between the blooms of ornamental grasses, repeating their angular lines. A few Japanese anemone dotted the display with button-shaped flowers. Even after the anemone drops its petals, its green button eyes light up bouquets.

Mexican sage has cashmere-soft purple calyxes that highlight the white angora flowers lining its stems. Combined with lime-green nicotiana, sapphire blue monkshood, and dark red roses, this beauty garners all the attention. It is also one of the best salvias for dried flower arrangements, as it dries naturally in the vase. I save the stems when I'm discarding a bouquet to use later on.

There are numerous other fall-blooming salvias, some with a 5-foot stature. These are especially useful in tall bouquets, but they can also be cut down to size to fit anywhere. Whatever their height, salvias exhibit changeable personalities. They can be sophisticated when consorting with roses and dahlias, yet very free-spirited dancing among ornamental grasses, fall foliage, and berries. They have strong stems that can be poked easily into floral foam.

Among the fall-blooming salvias, 'Indigo Spires' has deep violet blue flowers. The anise-scented sage is its rival for height, beauty, and continuous bloom. Its inflorescences are up to 10 inches long. 'Purple Majesty' sports a purple flower. Prairie sage is loved for the brightness and clarity of its azure blue blooms, a blue rarely seen in flowers. Brazilian bog sage, *S. uliginosa*, has lovely, densely spaced, pale blue flowers lining the top 6 inches of its gracefully arching stems. The gentian sage, *S. patens*, is slightly shorter, 3 feet tall or so, with deep blue 2-inch flowers that bloom in pairs. There is also a light blue variety named 'Cambridge Blue'. I could go on and on naming cultivars, but you get the picture. Now put down this book and order some!

Opposite: A bouquet with sweet gum leaves, dahlias, monkshood, pineapple sage, Mexican sage, and rose hips sparkles when lit from behind. Below: Mexican sage, monkshood, tobacco plant, and roses make an exuberant display.

Celebrating the Harvest

One of the greatest thrills of autumn is the vegetable harvest—and not just for cooks. I always scoop up some vegetables to include in arrangements, especially for my Thanksgiving buffet. Instead of a cornucopia, I lay a basket on its side, creating the illusion that its bounty is spilling out. It's an indulgence for the eyes, as splendid as the food being served, and an effective symbol for Thanksgiving: My harvest basket runneth over.

Opposite: A harvest basket of flowers, fruit, and vegetables. Below: A floral foam wreath on a cake stand covered in ornamental peppers and cherry tomatoes.

To make your own vegetable harvest basket, line the basket with aluminum foil to protect the table from water spills, then tape two moistened bricks of floral foam inside. Turn it on its side and poke in smoke-tinted burgundy and brown crape myrtle leaves and green berries; all effectively hide the foam. Salmon pink Sheffield mums can brighten the mix. Use assorted gourds, pumpkins, peppers, and apples and let them spill out across the table, creating an unforgettable floral and vegetable visual feast.

Ornamental peppers and cherry tomatoes are my personal favorites for fall displays. Since they're so abundant in October, I frequently mix them in with fall flowers. A floral foam wreath, covered with the velvety soft foliage of rose-scented geranium leaves and spiked with colorful peppers, is a perfect centerpiece for a Mexican dinner and a great way to celebrate the harvest. Elevated on a cake plate, a pepper wreath has pride of place.

Pumpkins are another staple for fall bouquets. Scooped out and fitted with a plastic liner and floral foam, pumpkins can be filled with an array of flowers and berries.

MUM'S THE WORD

Sheffield mums are pretty in salmon pink. With their yellow centers, they resemble daisies rather than typical mums, especially when they fade to white as they age. Sheffield mums are so floriferous, they bloom from early October until after heavy frost, 6 weeks or more later.

Although they are a little disconcerting at this time of year, defying as they do fall's palette of bright crayon colors, their pink color effortlessly mixes with other flowers. In the vase, Sheffield mums are my longest performers, lasting 3 weeks or more, long past the need for dusting. Each stem is its own bouquet, branching at the top into six to nine flowers. An arrangement of pink roses mixed with Sheffield mums, then inter-

spersed with the pink berries of the Korean mountain ash (*Sorbus alnifolia*), brightened up my living room mantle for a week. When the roses faded, the mums and berries carried on alone.

NAKED LADIES

Fall-blooming bulbs have their own distinct behavior. Two classics, the magic lily (*Lycoris squamigera*) and the autumn crocus, send up their foliage earlier in the year, with their flowers appearing in late summer or early fall. They are collectively known as "naked ladies," blooming undressed without their foliage.

The magic lily's long straplike leaves appear and disappear by midsummer; then its blooms show up a month or so later. Their appearance is triggered by a soaking rain, and they shoot up so quickly, it's like magic. The fragrant trumpet is 3 to 4 inches across and blooms in clusters of 8 to 12 flowers. Picking a few stems goes undetected in the garden, but sure makes a difference indoors. I like them with other late-summer bloomers: roses, crape myrtle, and phlox.

Colchicums, members of the Lily family, are easily confused with autumn-flowering crocus, members of the Iris family. Both flowers are commonly called autumn crocus and sport a similar wine-glass shape. Their color is best described as plum juice swirled into custard. For positive proof of what's what, count the stamens in the center of the flower: A colchicum has six stamens, while a crocus has three.

Still, colchicums are giants, more than twice the size of true crocus. The three most commonly grown are the double 'Waterlily' and the singles 'Lilac Wonder' and 'The Giant'. They are as simple to cultivate as daffodils and just as showy, so why are they so rarely seen in gardens? Is it because gardening wanes for many of us at the end of summer?

AT THE PEAK

Colorful foliage is fall's sunset. Truly, nothing broadcasts excitement like an inferno of red, yellow, and orange foliage. Leaves are the star attraction of many of my fall arrangements. Even when tempered by softer tones, these look-at-me hues come on strong. I cut and arrange the foliage the same way I do with any greens, removing all leaves growing below the waterline, recutting the stem on an angle, and supplementing the water with a floral preservative. (For details, see "Guidelines for Conditioning Flowers" on page 195.)

Since leaves morph over several months with trees and shrubs taking turns coloring up, I have new choices weekly, with a variety of shapes, sizes, and colors. There isn't a flower or a berry that doesn't want to strut its stuff against such a gloriously colored background. Wreaths, topiaries, branch bouquets, garlands, and flourishes for gifts all are quickly assembled from the wealth of turning leaves. But, no doubt about it, some foliage is better than others.

OPPOSITE: After the wire wreath frame was covered in oak leaves and Oriental bittersweet, it was sprayed with a matte shellac.

BUG OFF

Gardeners and floral designers can't be squeamish. More than once, I've discovered dozing bees gorging on the last bit of nectar between the petals of a dahlia or rose. When I'm arranging, I usually have a bucket of water nearby, so I can dunk and swish around the flower heads until the bee comes out. For a moment, the drenched bee can't fly. I spoon him out, carry him to the back door, and set him on the ground. Within minutes, he is dried and gone. Bees are "keepers." They are one of the reasons my flowers bloom. The only time a bee stings me is when I'm outdoors running barefoot through the clover and mistakenly step on one. Then we both cry.

Ants, centipedes, and beetles are another matter. When they emerge from a blossom, they are squashed or drowned—no qualms about it. Yet, when a ladybug wandered into my house on November 15, it touched my heart. I wanted to protect it, even though I didn't know how.

TOPS IN TREES

At their height of color, swamp and sugar maple leaves are a divine jumble of orange and yellow. Bunched in an earthenware pitcher with oak leaves, they deliver a quiet beauty. Add a half-dozen bright purple monkshood to the maples, and the display becomes eye-popping, setting a party mood. Japanese cutleaf maples are more delicate in shape, but the leaves, with a wash of red and yellow, are stunning. Pair these with berries, dahlias, and ageratum.

Oaks, on the other hand, occasionally disappoint us, turning a lifeless tan. But when nature cooperates, their spectrum can be glorious, ranging from honey, yellow, and red highlights on younger trees to richest russet on older specimens. One October, I taped a small oakleaf wreath and a gracefully curving branch across the window to admire its beauty up close, while watching the gardens undressing outdoors. Twigs of oak leaves poked into a straw wreath with bittersweet and Linden viburnum berries lasted for months. And I can't count the number of times I've relied on oak branches to fill in large arrangements. Often, since they're so top heavy, I attach the branches with waterproof floral tape to the back of the vase before I position the flowers and berries.

OPPOSITE: A simple arrangement of swamp maple and oak foliage with white berries as an accent. BELOW: A straw wreath at the peak of the porch has oak leaves, bittersweet, viburnum berries, and a lotus pod poked in.

I also adore sweetgum trees. When the sun streams through their branches, the trees glow pink. Yet, on close inspection, the leaves are a blend of colors—burgundy, yellow, orange, red, purple, and green—and just perfect to tuck into a vase. The small fruits are equally delightful, although you might question why, since they resemble spiky medieval weapons of war. Early in the season, before the leaves turn colors, the balls are bright lime green, vivacious in any arrangement. Later they blush to a ruddy brown, and lastly, they turn to tan. I collect them to add texture to holiday wreaths, and occasionally, I spray them with gold glitter so they sparkle.

SHRUBS AND MORE

Burning bush blazes from early September into smoldering ambers by mid-November. Picked at its peak, the leaves last for at least a week out of water and several weeks in it. Backing an arrangement, burning bush sends up red flames. Dark purple monkshood and the red feathered plumes of pineapple sage are vibrant enough to survive the heat. Brightly colored dahlias and roses add to the fun. In another arrangement, this time to douse the flames, I chose white roses and bugbane (*Cimicifuga simplex* 'White Pearl'), plus a crowd of pink crape myrtle seeds. Like much fall foliage, burning bush leaves are translucent, so I place them in a spot that makes them shimmer with backlight. Another plus to burning bush: The individual oval leaves can be mistaken for petals. When glued onto a gift-wrapped package in a daisy design with a strawflower "button" at its center, they create a present with presence (see page 97).

OPPOSITE, CLOCKWISE FROM TOP RIGHT: An antique fire bucket holds blueberry foliage, bittersweet, and berries. A wreath of leucothoe, nandina, and viburnum berries. Roses, crape myrtle, and burning bush with bugbane. Oakleaf hydrangea and Japanese maple branches mix with rose hips. BELOW: Cutting 'Wood's Dwarf' nandina.

Nandina domestica 'Wood's Dwarf' is a type of heavenly bamboo that rages scarlet in fall and on through winter. If I cut a stem as it starts to turn, there is a rich mix of red and green among the small elongated oval leaves. The leaves are compound,

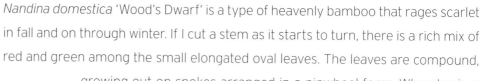

growing out on spokes arranged in a pinwheel form. When I snip a stem off, it doesn't even leave a hole in the shrub and it easily covers the top of a 12-inch-diameter bowl to form the basis of an arrangement. I often use a Chinese export bowl, picking up the porcelain's colors with roses, cup and saucer vine, and ageratum.

Just looking around the yard reveals other dazzling fall foliage. Witch hazel leaves resemble the plumes of a tropical bird, flaunting a yellow center with red feathering around the serrated edges. Oakleaf hydrangeas are tie-dyed with green, red, and yellow. Blueberry foliage sends up flames in yellow, pink, red, and deep burgundy, perfect to display in a fire bucket. Hosta leaves melt into marvelous gold patterns before dissolving as bright white skeletons, a terrific closing act.

SEEDPODS

Poppy, thistle, and lotus pods are superb on wreaths or combined with colorful foliage or ornamental grasses. Dried sunflower heads, packed with rounds of seeds, are themselves astonishing works of art. On a wreath, they are the center of attention. Hardy begonias' pink winged pods amuse viewers when dangled over the rim of a bouquet of flowers.

Clematis seedpods are fascinating spun-gold whorls. I use the golden pods in wreaths and in candle cups. If the seed heads are treated to stop them from turning into fluffy white strands and riding away on the wind, they last for months. I tried two different methods: spraying them lightly with shellac and putting their stems in glycerin. Both methods work. To try the glycerin system, mix two parts hot water to one part glycerin. (Glycerin is available at most drug stores and can be used again and again; just strain out any debris and reheat.) Put the stems of the seedpods into the mixture and leave them for a week or two. It takes that long for the glycerin to be absorbed up into the stems, which darken as it rises. The seedpod is ready to use when the glycerin has reached its top.

OPPOSITE: A bouquet of dried grass, forsythia foliage, bittersweet berries, sweetgum balls, and poppy seed heads. LEFT: Hardy begonia seedpods hang like fringe from a vase of dahlias, roses, monkshood, and more.

BERRY MADNESS

In fall, it is easy to have a merry time with berries. There are so many to choose from—from pearl-size rose hips to heavenly bamboo's grapelike clumps. Berries contrast with the bigger shapes of leaves and flowers in wreaths, candle cups, and bouquets. Think of them as tassels and let them dangle.

One of my top berry picks is *Ampelopsis brevipedunculata*, commonly called porcelain berry. A Grape family member, its berries hang in clusters of multicolored pastels with a finish that resembles a crackled glaze on porcelain. They combine beautifully with any plants, but they especially pair nicely with dahlias and roses. In candle cups, they are marvelous dangling down and are easily seen. However, with something so beautiful there is always a catch: Porcelain berry is a thug. It grows in a wild part of my garden, but I don't recommend it for a small bed, because it is so invasive. I cut mine back yearly. Along the roadside, if unchecked, it blankets small trees and shrubs.

I don't recommend inviting Oriental bittersweet *(Celastrus orbiculatus)* into your garden, either, although it has berries cherished for wreaths. It is an invasive plant, outlawed in many states, so I do my part to keep it in bounds. I collect it along the roadside and on the beach.

Bittersweet's burnished colors go with everything. Picked and laid on a mantle or table or wound around a wreath, the vines look good for months. When designing with them, I cut off some or all of the leaves to expose the berries. As the yellow berries open, they dry and expose bright orange centers.

Another dangerous orange-red beauty is firethorn. The tightly clustered berries invite gazing, but cutting them from this shrub can be painful. Its thorns grab and don't want to let go, so wearing iron gloves is appropriate. Because of firethorn's compact nature, you'll find so many berries clustered together that they easily cover a floral form. I wired scores of clusters onto a large metal frame. The square wreath was stunning, more noticeable than if it had been round.

That said, there are few fruiting shrubs that can compare with beautyberry. Its bright rosy purple berries are closely packed, lining each stem. Once the shrub loses its leaves, the berries are visible from a distance—and also when placed in an arrangement. I cut long stems and use them in floral bouquets.

We must not overlook the ornamental cherries' and the crabapples' dangling berries in red or orange, nor viburnums' red clusters. Any or all of these work!

PRESERVING FALL FOLIAGE

The leaves may be gone from the trees by Thanksgiving, but that doesn't mean I stop using them. After a windy day, I pick branches up off the ground, elated by the fact that the foliage is naturally air dried and not at all damaged. How they can survive a storm is a mystery, but I'll take them. Following one such blowdown, I made a garland of oak leaves, wiring small bunches to a rope. The garland hung on the porch railing for 6 weeks under an oakleaf wreath.

If the leaves are not completely dry, I may put their stems in water; their leaves will continue to dry more slowly. Sometimes I flatten whole branches, laying them between newspapers on a table in the garage and covering them with a heavy rug or storage boxes of books. A similar trick works with Boston ivy: I clip the leaves in their bright red stage and slip them into an old telephone book.

I also reuse foliage that I've placed in arrangements, since most leaves will hold their shape and dry naturally in a vase. Once they are crisp and dry, like paper to the touch, I give them a spray of shellac. I prefer a matte finish to a satin finish; a shine just looks unnatural. Sometimes I spray the leaves before I arrange them, but at other times, especially with wreaths, I spray the finished design.

OPPOSITE: A mock topiary decorated with rose hips and bittersweet among the maple and sweetgum leaves. Reindeer moss hides the base. BELOW: A garland of assorted leaves and berries wired around a rope base.

Another appealing way to decorate with dried leaves is to glue them onto tin cans and finish them with a spray of shellac. These unique containers can be used to carry bouquets to friends and neighbors. I have also used green iris foliage in this way, and it held up without any problems. Just more proof that foliage is fabulous!

GARDEN TIPS FOR FALL

• Invest in fall perennials. Most summer perennials blossom for only a few weeks. Fall bloomers—monkshood, hardy ageratum, salvias, and Japanese anemone among them—keep their flowers coming for months. Check to see what works in your area and purchase by mail order or at local nurseries. Most fall perennials can be planted in spring, summer, or fall, whenever you find them for sale.

• After the first killing frost, dig up dahlia tubers for winter storage. Each spring, cut the oldest tubers apart before replanting them. There are plenty to give away. Dahlias are one of the most giving plants.

• Sages, with their brightly colored flowers, stiff stems, and scented foliage, are butterfly and hummingbird magnets. Because of its running rootstock, anise-scented sage becomes a large patch in a few years in areas where winters stay above 10°F.

• Sheffield mums grow without fussing in my heavy clay soil, their clumps spreading by underground runners. I've lopped off a clump for almost everyone in the neighborhood. Monarch butterflies, too, are happy with my choice and flock to the salmon pink flowers.

• The same species of trees or shrubs growing near each other don't always color up at the same time or in exactly the same way. I have a sweetgum near my driveway that has bright color for 2 weeks or more before another one 30 feet away shows any color at all. So, enjoy fall's surprises!

• When fall leaves burst into color, and shrubs and vines are covered in berries, it's time to prune and to use the branches, foliage, and berries for bouquets. (Why prune in a season when the cuttings would just lie on your compost heap?)

OPPOSITE: A birdbath holds an arrangement of dried hydrangea and rose buds and hips. LEFT: A copper cone displays an array of dried grass, bugbane, Japanese anemone, and pineapple sage.

A hanging basket and an urn are filled with branches of inkberry, euonymus, and redtwig dogwood, plus dried yarrow that was spray-painted red. The garland was made of overlapping branches of euonymus wired together.

Winter's Wonders

Winter takes us back to the garden's bare essentials, when there's a quiet beauty in textures and shapes. At this time of year, bright color appears in little doses: golden conifers, holly berries, heavenly bamboo's blushing foliage, and pieris buds. Yet, winter is the season with the most surprises and miracles. Unique patterns and designs form when the snow falls and the wind blows. Mother Nature's one-of-a-kind flourishes painted in frost and sculpted in ice are thrilling. Like me, Nature isn't tidy. Winter is a messy season, and the garden gets disheveled. But I look for the wonders of winter and I always find goodies for snipping.

WINTER FAVORITES AT A GLANCE

Winter is the season of subtle colors in myriad textures and tones. In early winter I keep my bouquets coming by using evergreens in coats of many colors. My secret weapons for bright color are nandina and pieris. Both stay all winter in the garden and are long lasting in bouquets. By the end of winter, I do crave spring's first blooms. Witch hazel, snowdrops, hellebores, crocus, scilla, and other little bulbs that struggle through inclement weather to bring us their joyous blooms are the most welcome flowers of the year. They signal the garden is about to be reborn once again. I couldn't be without them.

FLOWERS

Aconite, winter (*Eranthis hyemalis*)

Crocus (*Crocus* sp.)

Daffodils (*Narcissus* sp.)

Glory of the snow (*Chionodoxa luciliae*)

Hellebores (*Helleborus* sp.)

Iris, dwarf (*Iris reticulata*)

Mahonia, leatherleaf or Oregon grape holly (*Mahonia*)

Pieris (*Pieris japonica*)

Snowdrops (*Galanthus* sp.)

Squill, striped (*Puschkinia scilloides*)

Viburnum, Bodnant hybrid (*Viburnum* x *bodnantense* 'Dawn')

Winter hazel, spike (*Corylopsis spicata*)

Witch hazel (*Hamamelis* sp.)

FOLIAGE

Bamboo, heavenly (*Nandina domestica*)

Bamboo, dwarf heavenly (*Nandina domestica* 'Wood's Dwarf')

Cypress, golden threadleaf false or Hinoki cypress (*Chamaecyparis obtusa* 'Crippsii')

Cypress, variegated false (*Chamaecyparis pisifera* 'Compacta Variegata')

Euonymus, variegated (*Euonymus* sp.)

Fir, Fraser (*Abies fraseri*)

Fir, noble (*Abies procera*)

Holly, false (*Osmanthus heterophyllus* 'Goshiki')

Inkberry (*Ilex glabra*)

Ivy, golden heart (*Hedera helix* 'Gold Heart')

Lavender (*Lavandula* sp.)

Leucothoe, drooping or Fetterbush (*Leucothoe fontanesiana* or *L. walteri*)

Magnolia, Southern (*Magnolia grandiflora*)

Pine, dragon's-eye (*Pinus densiflora* 'Oculus Draconis')

Pine, Eastern white (*Pinus strobus*)

Spruce, blue (*Picea pungens*)

Spruce, oriental (*Picea orientalis* 'Skylands')

BERRIES AND SEED HEADS

Allium (*Allium aflatunense*)

Holly (*Ilex* sp. and hybrids)

Rose hips (*Rosa* sp.)

Winterberry (*Ilex verticillata*)

OPPOSITE: A cone of floral foam is covered in assorted greens including blue spruce and golden threadleaf cypress. A dried allium seed head sprayed white and covered in glitter is the gong.

Waking Up the Garden

Instead of putting the garden to bed for winter, I wake it up. Besides the usual holiday fare— wreaths on the doors and garlands around the windows—I treat both obvious and tucked- away spots to some new finery. Containers, window boxes, and hanging baskets are lush with bouquets of boughs. Outdoor tables sport winter coats and a bare limb might dangle a greenery bell. The birdbaths and benches are clad in clipped fir, the appropriate dress for the season. All winter the garden looks like it is lived in and enjoyed.

To make all this happen, I've declared that "December is for pruning"—everything from buds to berries, boxwood to conifers. (I carefully balance what I cut to assure the garden doesn't look like a bad haircut.) The more mature the plant, the more I snip. Evergreens are the first plants I visit; they're the staples for both indoor and outdoor arrangements. Snippings easily last for months in the cold air. (Cool air temperature is the most important factor in prolonging the life of cut greens and flowers.)

But being the confirmed flower lover that I am, for a long time I never gave other foliage plants much attention. Then one winter when flowers were few, I began assembling arrangements solely of different leaves. It was an awakening. Leaves

come in endless guises, revealing the amazing intricacies of nature: filigreed (heavenly bamboo and chamaecyparis), leathery (magnolia and rhododendron), and spiky (yucca and holly). As for color possibilities, the range is astounding, from blue spruce and golden conifers to red nandina 'Wood's Dwarf' and tie-dyed *Leucothoe fontanesiana* 'Rainbow', awaiting those who seek them out.

For starters, think of texture as a way to introduce depth to a green-on-green scheme. Hairy, leathery, matte, prickly, puckered, saw-toothed, silky, smooth, velvety—there's a seemingly endless category of leaves. In fact, once you start truly noticing plant texture, you'll discover that it can be used as creatively as color. Think tapestries!

OPPOSITE: Winterberries and rose hips add bright color to a container of rhododendron branches and other greens. ABOVE: A hanging basket has branches of inkberry and euonymus, and dried yarrow spray-painted red, poked in.

Try glossy against wrinkled and silky against feathery—the juxtaposition emphasizes the primary characteristics of each. Texture can also define a mood. Lacy foliage, as in chamaecyparis, almost automatically looks romantic, ethereal, old-fashioned. Big, deeply veined or glossy leaves like magnolia and rhododendron convey an aura of voluptuousness. Anything fuzzy, hairy, or velvety smooth like lamb's ear beckons to be touched, adding a sensuality you could never produce with color alone.

Once you get the knack of playing with texture, you can arrange almost anything, indoors or out. For now, let's consider my "dress up the garden" theme.

FINESSING THE FURNITURE

OPPOSITE: An urn filled with branches of euonymus, inkberry, redtwig dogwood, and punctuated with red dried yarrow. **ABOVE:** An outdoor "tablescape" with a bird's nest filled with cranberries and surrounded by magnolia leaves and rose hips.

Our outdoor benches, tables, and chairs remain in place all year so the garden doesn't look empty and unloved and I give them a winter flourish. On a mild day, I enjoy sitting in the garden. Or at least knowing I can. Lately, I've taken a crazy turn by "setting" the outdoor tables with centerpieces or runners of greens—and even hanging an evergreen bell as a chandelier and adding a decorative spray to the back of a bench—to create a fairyland for Mother Nature to play in. And play she does! She hangs icicles from the bell and dusts the tables with snow and ice. The decorated tables perk up our view. It looks like guests are expected to a winter party.

Last year, I created a centerpiece for a small round table using a bird's nest nestled among a fan of magnolia leaves. The nest had blown out of a tree the day before. A rectangular table showed off a runner of blue spruce embellished with clusters of heavenly bamboo berries and gold pinecones. After I completed these simple table decorations, I decided to make a green tapestry with a bell-shaped chandelier above it. For the tapestry, I laid noble fir branches around the table like spokes on a wheel, then ruffled the table's edge with pieris. The center was filled with berries, false holly, holly, and pinecones.

I formed the chandelier around a floral foam cone wrapped with chicken wire. At the bottom, the stiff cuttings of blue spruce shaped the bell outward, as gold and green chamaecyparis draped provocatively down the sides. Using an allium seed head saved from summer, I spray-painted it white and frosted it with glitter to mimic a gong. A few pinecones wired on top helped to cinch it in and shape the bell where it was attached to the wire holder and hung from a tree limb.

TURNS ON AN URN

Nothing looks lonelier than an empty pot in a scantily clad winter garden. It sends the message: "Something is missing." Consequently, I fill up frost-proof containers—cement, fiberglass, and metal—with evergreens and berries, arranged like large bouquets.

Boughs are poked into moist soil instead of into floral foam. The soil holds the stems in place and supplies them with moisture. These outdoor decorations take little time to make, yet last for months. As winter progresses, they freeze and are frosted with snow and ice. This makes the view out my windows enchanting, and I grin like the fat cat that swallowed the bird, especially when I'm sitting beside a blazing fire.

FOLIAGE FAVORITES

Topping my list of foliage plants for winter color is nandina 'Wood's Dwarf', a heavenly bamboo. (There are other similar cultivars, such as 'Firepower'.) Its bright scarlet leaves ignite any arrangement. I have a cluster of a half-dozen plants, but they grow so slowly I fall on my knees in front of them to beg them to sprout faster. At 3 years old, my plants are only 2 feet high (they'll eventually hit about 4 feet), but plump enough that I have a ready supply of stems. I often display 'Wood's Dwarf' alone in a floral foam wreath centerpiece. It is hard to believe, but

one wreath I put together in early December still looked good a month later, because the foliage dried slowly, holding its shape and color. Mixed with other items, nandina takes me through winter. It's the perfect partner for pieris, whose natural stance is peering over an edge. And 'Wood's Dwarf' is the only flourish needed for a low narrow runner of evergreens to top a dining table or a fireplace mantle.

To make a runner for a table or a mantle, place a brick of moist floral foam on a low oval platter or tray. Add a long branch tip of noble fir to each end and shorter tips along the sides. To make the pieces poke easily into the foam and to keep them fresh in water, cut each on a slant and remove its needles 1 inch from the end. This is a necessary step before inserting any conifer into floral foam or water. Then build the arrangement, layering from the

outer edges to the inside. The foliage should be dense enough to completely hide the platter and foam. The evergreens last for almost 3 weeks in floral foam, if the foam is kept moist. You can also accessorize the arrangement with flowers from the market, which usually last 5 to 7 days.

Drooping leucothoe, a colonizing evergreen shrub, sends up gracefully arching red stems from its base. The stems reach 3 to 6 feet high with dark green shiny leaves lining each branch. Cold weather causes the leaves to blush and blotch with burgundy. 'Scarletta' has a dark purple winter hue, and 'Girard's Rainbow' is tie-dyed with streaks of gold, lime green, pink, and red. Both are colorful additions to arrangements or containers. Add some winterberries, pieris, and cotoneaster for a lively display.

OPPOSITE: Winterberry, pieris, and leucothoe complement each other in a vase.
ABOVE: A brick of floral foam is elongated with clippings of blue Atlas cedar, blue spruce, golden tips of Oriental spruce 'Skylands', and variegated holly. Nandina 'Wood's Dwarf' fills the center.

GARDEN GLITTER

Gold foliage is a rare natural resource, certainly in the floral market. All the more reason to plant some sunny-toned shrubs to gild winter displays. Golden thread-leaf false cypress (*Chamaecyparis obtusa* 'Crippsii') has finely textured, lacy foliage that glows brightly year 'round. It has so much pizzazz, it can strut its stuff in a basket filled with floral foam and only needs a holiday bow tied to the handle to be fancied up as a hostess present. In mixed arrangements outdoors or indoors, it gracefully drapes down over the edge of its container. Oriental spruce 'Skylands' is another splendid choice. Its golden branches scoop down as the tips curve up. I use large sprays of 'Skylands' in outdoor containers and its tips in wreaths and

arrangements. The tip sprays are perfectly formed to cradle nosegays on holiday presents. Naughty but nice, the false holly *Osmanthus heterophyllus* 'Goshiki' is a bit prickly, but its new growth is mesmerizing, speckled with spots of color like bronze, gold, green, and pink. You need to handle it with care to avoid the thorns, but it can't be beat for perking up wreaths and arrangements. Dragon's-eye pine, *Pinus densiflora* 'Oculus Draconis', might be unpronounceable, but the wide strips of yellow on its 5-inch green needles make it a standout. Employ it wherever you need a Midas touch.

OPPOSITE: A basket of *Chamaecyparis* 'Crippsii' and rose hips. LEFT: Presents topped with a variegated holly wreath, a spray-painted allium, and a nosegay of Oriental spruce 'Skylands' and rose hips.

WREATHING THE SEASON

Wreaths are a Christmas tradition, traditionally hung on doors, garden gates, and windows, but there are so many more places to show them off. And there are infinite combinations of berries, dried flowers, foliage, and seed heads to combine in them. Although unexpected in a garden setting, a wreath around the outer rim of a birdbath fits like a fir shawl, dressing it appropriately for the season. Wreaths are also enchanting when topping containers of dried ornamental grass or even surrounding candles.

To save time and effort, I purchase plain Fraser fir wreaths and garlands that I personalize by wiring on distinctive adornments—golden conifers, nandina 'Wood's Dwarf', pieris, and variegated hollies—just about anything I find in the garden. Once I'm finished, each creation is one of a kind and no longer a cliché. This really is the easiest way to create something unique.

Hanging wreaths indoors is a nice touch, but I try to avoid pounding nails into my walls. So I was delighted to find in a holiday catalog some metal stands that hold a wreath upright on a table or mantle instead. I camouflage the base and pole of the stand with ribbons and ornaments so the wreath looks like it's floating.

For my New Year's party centerpiece, Tracy Vivona, the floral designer of Designs by T. Alexandria in Oyster Bay, New York, picked sprigs of conifers from my garden and poked them into a floral foam wreath. She combined blue spruce, variegated chamaecyparis, dragon's-eye pine, golden false cypress, and white pine. Purchased lilies, roses, white hydrangea, and a glittery candle completed the gorgeous wintery wreath. After a week, the flowers wilted and were tossed out, but the conifer base looked good for another 3 weeks. I gussied it up with berries and pieris from my garden.

Although classic wreaths are round, other shapes—snowflakes, squares, stars, and trees—are available in wire forms and just as easily covered with greens. Bunches of leaves and conifers overlapping in the same direction are wired on until the metal is completely hidden. Berries and rose hips lend a finishing touch.

A snowflake frame gleams when covered with blue Atlas cedar, its short stiff needles bursting from the stem in fetching rosettes. The powder-blue fir, dusted with silver, sparkles just like the real thing. A star base is another alternative. Decked in holiday colors—green boxwood clippings topped by red rose hips—it sends the season's message in a brand new way. A tree form is perfectly at home, too, covered with white-pine bristles and winterberry ornaments. An allium seed head, sprayed white, acts as a garden angel on top. The tree's trunk is a small log, stood on end and slit at the top so that the tree form could be slipped into it to stand alone. Other years, the tree form was captivating hanging on a door.

Mini wreaths are another festive way to go. I make a few small enough to hang on doorknobs or decorate presents (see page 130). Holiday gifts embellished with a wreath, swag, or a natural ornament is the equivalent of two presents in one.

OPPOSITE: A garland and wreath made from an assortment of greens: rhododendron, magnolia, golden conifers, pinecones, ivy, blue spruce, and winterberries. BELOW: A caged brick of floral foam holds a spray of greens, berries, and dried rosebuds.

GARNISHING GARLANDS

Wreaths and garlands go together, especially on a front door. For a Christmas garland, I usually start with a ready-made Fraser fir or princess pine garland and then embellish it. To surround my front door, I need one 20 feet long. Once the garland is hung in place, I wire on an assortment of other foliage, including golden conifers, berries, pinecones, and occasionally ribbons. Even though I'm standing on a ladder to decorate it, it is easier to see from there where a bit of gold or red is needed to balance the look.

Making Mini Trees

Often sold in flower shops, miniature boxwood Christmas trees are a holiday fixture I can't live without. However, because they're so expensive, I make them myself. I cut a brick of floral foam into a triangle and stand it on end. Then I poke in 4- or 5-inch cuttings of boxwood at the top of the tree and immediately skip to the bottom to insert more pieces. It is easier to fill in the middle once the top and bottom are in place. Once finished, I place my tree on a "trunk," a 5- or 6-inch section cut from a small log. Although boxwood is the classic mini-tree choice, I often mix it with different types of foliage. For a golden tree, golden threadleaf false cypress works well and rose hips add a bit more color. Variegated pines and mixed green foliage are other variations. Dried flowers, especially hydrangea, make interesting mini trees as well. Experiment with your favorites. You will be surprised at how easy it is.

OPPOSITE, CLOCKWISE FROM TOP RIGHT: **Mini trees made with boxwood; variegated conifer; dried hydrangeas; and golden threadleaf false cypress and 'Goshiki' osmanthus.** BELOW: **Holly and magnolia leaves snuggle into glasses filled with cranberries.**

Berry Merry Holiday

Winterberries, the deciduous hollies, grow in large luscious bunches, without prickly leaves or thorns to discourage your foraging. By late November, my bushes are covered in berries, but if I don't pick the scarlet fruit quickly, the birds gobble them up, and I'm forced to buy bunches. Consequently, I've stooped to playing hide-and-seek with the birds, planting winterberries in out-of-the-way places. One snuggles behind a clump of hydrangeas, contributing nothing to my garden's design—but its berries are safely tucked away from avian thieves.

Eventually the birds find it, but usually after I have picked my fill. Winterberries are colorful additions to outdoor containers, wreaths, indoor bouquets—you name it. They top my list of berries for holiday fare. A particular favorite is 'Winter Red', with its profusion of berries.

Not planted as often are the orange and yellow winterberries: 'Aurantiaca' has abundant orange fruit, and 'Chrysocarpa' has yellow. The birds often ignore these berries until late winter when they are short of food, so I can pick them until March. They remain colorful in the winter landscape and add color to bouquets and wreaths.

Evergreen hollies hold their berries longer than winterberries, so I don't need to be quite as cunning—or as quick with the collecting. Perhaps their thorns thwart mass feasting by the birds. Out a bedroom window one lazy morning, I watched a bird enjoying a leisurely meal, resting and fluffing his feathers between bites. And happily, my hollies are large enough that any snipping does not deprive the birds of breakfast. But sometimes those fetching fruits, so eye-catching on the bush, get lost in a bouquet. An easy way to direct the focus to the berries is to display them with more berries. In this case, cranberries. I filled three wine glasses with cranberries and water, paraded them down the center of the table, then poked in magnolia and holly branches. Just like marbles or pebbles, the cranberries hold the plant stems in place; they're also a marvelous way to add color to a clear container, since they won't decay.

The birds rarely touch heavenly bamboo's hard crimson berries. They hang at the top of the stem in large clusters like grapes. The berries last both indoors and out for months, only fading slightly. The bamboolike evergreen foliage is tipped with red and turns redder as the season progresses. It's attractive with or without the berries in candle cups and other displays.

WINTER-FLOWERING SHRUBS

OPPOSITE: The fragrant blooms of Oregon grape holly mixed with *Helleborus foetidus* brighten a winter day. BELOW: Branches of witch hazel combined with the green flowers of *Helleborus foetidus*.

As winter winds down, cheerful yellow blooms spring up on Cornelian cherry (*Cornus mas*), Oregon grape holly (*Mahonia*), winter hazel, and witch hazel. Viburnum 'Dawn' and pieris blossoms open in softer colors of pink and white. These shrubs glory in bad weather. That's all they've ever known. They are my winter solace.

My three witch hazels, 'Arnold Promise', 'Diane', and 'Jelena', bloom in early to mid-winter and perfume the air. Their spidery blooms are thick and waxy, protecting them from frost, rain, and snow. Witch hazels have staying power. In 2008-2009, the coldest winter in 10 years, 'Arnold Promise' flowered from late January into April. Cold invigorates and prolongs the bloom; warm weather hurries it on its way. 'Jelena', with coppery orange blooms, is usually the first to flaunt flowers, followed by the ruby red 'Diane'. They are all distinctively scented—not sweet, but pleasant enough. Neither 'Jelena' nor 'Diane' sticks around as long as 'Arnold Promise', so if you can only plant one, Arnold's your man.

Putting a bundle of mixed colors of witch hazel branches into a tall vase always makes me pause to realize how lucky I am to have these winter bloomers so close at hand. And when hellebores blossom, a few stems of the lime green flowers of *Helleborus foetidus*

work as a focal point at the base of witch hazel branches. Blooming later are the season's straddlers, fair-weather shrubs that wait for warmer temperatures to flower—sometimes in March, sometimes in April. No matter, they are worth the wait. Spike winter hazel, one of the most elegant shrubs, usually gets going in March. It grows wider than tall, eventually reaching 6 feet, with clusters of soft yellow bells that emit a sweet cowslip fragrance. Each flower blooms several inches from its neighbor, so if you cut between the blooms, you can pretty much cut flowers sized to fit any container. I mix the stems with early daffodils and hellebores.

Mahonia bears spiky, shiny green leaves surrounding compressed panicles of yellow flowers, followed by large clusters of blue-black berries; hence its common name, Oregon grape holly. Once the flower buds show color, it looks sophisticated paired with the lime green blooms of the "stinking hellebore," *Helleborus foetidus* (see page 141). And yes, it does stink, but only if you stick your nose right into a bloom—and why would you do that?

Not as showy as the witch hazels, Bodnant hybrid viburnums have pink or white tassels borne on naked stems, often several feet apart. 'Dawn' is a sweetly scented bright pink hybrid that blooms along our woodland path. It is a cheery sight. I cut off lower branches and clip them apart, so each flower cluster is on a short stem. Then I can pair them with snowdrops. They also last longer on shorter stems.

The dangling green buds of pieris hang like seed pearls from rosettes of small leaves in fall. By winter, the buds color up in red, pink, or white. Cut foliage and buds last for 2 weeks or more indoors and longer out, adding texture and color to arrangements, containers, and wreaths. The tasseled flowers contrast especially well with the open cups of hellebores. For an elegant dinner table arrangement, the two make a lovely couple in candle cups. On a 13-candle candelabra, I stuck moistened Mini-Deco holders (little domes of floral foam on peel-and-stick plastic bases) over five of the candle cups. It was easy to poke flowers into the holders, instantly transforming an ordinary candelabra into a floral fantasy.

EARLY-BLOOMING BULBS

Early bloomers like dwarf iris, glory of the snow, snowdrops, and winter aconite may be small, but they light up the garden in a big way. While other plants are still asleep, these petite charmers tiptoe in ever so quietly to steal the show. If you have never planted these demure beauties, you're in for a pleasant surprise. They're inexpensive, easy to grow, and they work double time multiplying to spread their beauty. They cast their seeds about after they bloom and at the same time form baby bulbs underground.

Opposite: Wine glasses sport bunches of pink and blue glory of the snow and pushkinia. **Below:** Shot glasses hold glory of the snow, crocus, pansies, dwarf iris, and snowdrops.

The symbolic value of winter flowers and their stamina should not be taken for granted. If a snowdrop isn't put on Earth as a hopeful sign that all things are possible, what is? It is so tiny a bloom, yet so vigorous and so capable. It is impossible not to admire its ruggedness. These petite bloomers are seemingly impervious to the weather. Although they are tiny blooms on short stems, averaging 6 inches in height, they make a big impact at this time of year, both indoors and out.

The common snowdrop *Galanthus nivalis* naturalized in my lawn and woodland. The giant snowdrop *G. elwesii*, with its larger flower and 10-inch stem, has colonized a corner of my flower border. A crowd of frilly doubles, 'Flore Pleno', blooms above the pachysandra. These snowdrops' stems can be as tall as 11 inches late in the season when they have stretched up to their full height. In the house, they are at their best radiating out from a vase, so that their three droopy white rabbit-ear-shaped petals stand out. Inside each bloom are another three shorter petals each tipped with green. But even the most diminutive snowdrops can steal the scene. Certainly it was true of the snowdrops I hung in a rattan glove on

OPPOSITE, RIGHT: Snowdrops, glory of the snow, and dwarf iris atop a candlestick. OPPOSITE, LEFT: Snowdrops in a water glass hidden in a wicker glove. ABOVE: A nosegay of winter aconite and dwarf iris wrapped with a yucca leaf.

the front door. Their stems were in a plastic water bottle hidden inside the glove. They stayed fresh for over a week in the cold air.

Winter aconite comes along next, usually in February, with golden chalices glistening above ruffled collars of foliage. As the corms mature, they send up more flowers. I dug up a clump of nine blooms, planning to divide them, only to discover they were all coming from one walnut-size corm. That's one hardworking guy. The blooms stay for a few weeks, departing before the snowdrops do, and their bright sunny hue is a welcome addition to bouquets.

Once the snowdrops and winter aconite open, crocus, dwarf iris, glory of the snow, and striped squill follow close behind. Crocus stems are so short, 4 to 5 inches, that they need a shallow bowl or even a shot glass to strut their stuff indoors. The bright blue of dwarf iris livens up any petite bouquet. Glory of the snow is a 6-inch gem with 8 to 10 flowers per stem. Unlike other early bloomers, they don't nod

their heads. Rather, they turn their chins up to the sky, letting us gaze directly into their violet blue flowers punctuated with white centers. Striped squill wear the faded blue of denim. Although they, too, are short, they make their presence known with numerous flowers lining their 5- to 6-inch stems.

As these plucky little blooms appear, I mix them together in mini bouquets. Sometimes I bundle them into a nosegay, secure it with a rubber band, and then wrap a lance-shaped leaf from a golden yucca as if it were a ribbon around the stems. Other times, I take advantage of their short stems, which can be a challenge, by tucking them into jelly glasses, shot glasses, teacups, votives, and even old perfume bottles. Here, the small snips are totally endearing. But sometimes I want to raise them up where they can be better seen. Displayed in wine glasses, the short-stemmed blooms appear taller. The cup of a candlestick, if it holds a few inches of water, also does the trick. Or, grouped in a plastic vial and poked into floral foam between greens, the vial adds inches to their height, like elevator shoes for bulbs.

Hooray for Hellebores

Wouldn't you think that an easygoing perennial that blooms from mid-winter to June and colonizes vigorously, leaving yearly gifts of baby seedlings, would be found in most American gardens? Yet hellebores are not prevalent in the United States. Perhaps it is because designers' doubles are marketed at top prices. I planted six *Helleborus* hybrids a decade ago and now I have a hillside of single bloomers in an assortment of shades of white, pink, and purples. Their bracts subtly contrast with their showy yellow stamens. By late spring, the bracts, no matter what color they were when they first bloomed, have faded to light green, a color that works in every arrangement.

OPPOSITE AND BELOW: Pieris buds and hellebore blooms make wonderful indoor winter arrangements.

Freshly opened hellebore flowers can be capricious, lasting anywhere from a day to a week. Once cut, I've noticed that sometimes the ends of their stems close up and shrink to look like mouse tails. Cutting the stems right before putting them into water helps to eliminate this. To assure they last, I check the stems daily to see if they need recutting. If you notice the flowers wilting, recut the stems, put them in hot water for a minute, and refrigerate for a minimum of 6 hours. The flowers will revive and last for many more days. Once the bracts have faded to green, they last longer. Floating in water in shallow bowls or sherbet glasses, the flower heads last a week or more. In fact, this is one of my favorite ways to show them off, because you can look directly into their freckled faces.

GARDEN TIPS FOR WINTER

- Scoop up hellebore seedlings that sprout at the edge of their mother's skirt in spring and replant somewhere else. The babies usually have no trouble on their own, and in a few years, will have yet another generation that you can move again.

- If the pyramidal top of golden threadleaf false cypress is pruned, the plant assumes an ottoman shape in a dense mound. I planted several in a row and let them grow into a rounded hedge.

- While all of the early-blooming bulbs naturalize easily, they will only do so if you never cut back any of their foliage until it yellows and dies. The leaves are essential to allow photosynthesis to take place to replenish every bulb's nutrients.

- Bulbs can be planted as a petticoat around a shrub, to bloom with it or before it leafs out. Early and mid-season ones, such as snowdrops, winter aconite, and Siberian squill, placed close to the base of a lilac can enjoy full sun before the lilac puts out leaves. The golden flowers of forsythia are never so spectacular when amid blue Siberian squill or glory of the snow. Both the yellow flowers of leatherleaf mahonia and the pink or coral of flowering quince sparkle in a sea of grape hyacinth.

- When poised on an Oriental carpet of flowers, trees take on a more regal bearing. A witch hazel looks its best with early bulbs below: Clumps of snowdrops, early daffs, and Siberian squill settle in and keep the show going for years.

- Because of their small size, small bulbs must be planted in profusion for a fine show. A dozen is a drop in the bucket; a few hundred, a good beginning. But don't panic! Your back won't break, nor will you find your fingers worked to the bone. These end-of-winter warriors need only to be poked a few inches into the ground. The smaller the bulb, the more shallowly it's planted. A general rule is to plant to a depth three times the diameter of the bulb.

- Lawns are boring! There, I've said it. Dig up a patch of turf in a corner of your lawn and fold it back just enough to scatter a dozen bulbs under it. Then press the sod back into place, step on it, and water the bulbs in. It's that easy to turn a lawn into a closely cropped meadow—a delight for all the senses.

- Conifers come in all sizes, from dwarfs to giants, so no matter the size of your garden, there is always room for another.

- Every garden is a game of chance, each plant a gamble. Accept that and you'll have more fun!

OPPOSITE: An evergreen wreath rims the edge of a birdbath. It is decorated with berries, redtwig dogwood, and pinecones.

PART 2

Tricks of the Trade

A ball of floral foam is taped into a candle cup.
A candle, roses, and honeysuckle are poked in.

Roses wired on a green ribbon
make a stunning hat band.

PUTTING IT TOGETHER

When designing floral arrangements, my heart rules my head. I never concern myself with what is in or out of fashion. Flowers are timeless beauties. They outshine their surroundings when they are encouraged to be themselves. But flowers are not the whole story. Fruits, vegetables, berries, seedpods, all kinds of foliage, and even bare branches add seasonal interest and beauty to an arrangement. So while walking through the garden to collect cuttings, I pick what I like, gathering both the expected and the unexpected.

DETAILS ON DESIGN

Aside from designing a centerpiece so it doesn't obstruct the view of the person sitting across the table, I don't believe in rules for arranging flowers. Sure, proportion and balance are important, but stopping to measure the vase and the size of the bouquet is a waste of time. You'll miss all the fun. Amassing flowers to stand twice the height of the vase is an old design trick that works every time, but so does creating a dome of flowers atop a tall vase or completely hiding a low rectangular vessel with blooms hanging over the edge.

In fact, the only adage I follow is to let the flowers speak for themselves. If a vine spills out, a blossom leans, or a stem twists, I encourage it. I keep each flower's individuality in mind—like the soldier-straight zinnia stem or the sweet pea with a curve like a puppy's tail. I wouldn't try to loosen the stance or straighten the tail. If foliage and flowers drape over the rim of a vase or bowl, they soften the hard edge of the container, blurring the dividing line.

PAINTING WITH NATURE'S PALETTE

One Thanksgiving, I remember receiving a huge bouquet crammed with every color of flower under the sun. The blossoms were not carefully positioned, and their colors clashed, creating chaos. I pulled all the flowers out and segregated them with their own kind in different vases. Then I placed the vases down the center of the table in an orderly procession of colors. The effect was splendid, and it certainly taught me about the power of color: It can make or break an arrangement.

Color is the most immediate consideration for any bouquet. Flowers bloom in a veritable paint box of hues. Making a floral color wheel reinforced my belief that when combining all the available colors in an arrangement there needs to be an orderly progression of colors. When blossoms are plentiful, it is tempting to add one of everything to the vase. But if you do, it won't be a satisfying grouping. Trust me, I've tried. Too much of a good thing is confusing. Your eyes dart back and forth, not knowing where to look.

Another way to play with color is to think in terms of bright or subdued. I dither between the two, but who cares? Both can be gorgeous. Bright color stimulates and excites our senses. It appears to come forward to meet us. If you want an arrangement to dominate the room, go for a fiery mix of hot colors. Consider the neon orange of Mexican sunflowers, the brazen scarlet of roses, the screaming yellow of calendula, and the flamingo pink of many dianthus; these are known as the "60-miles-per-hour flowers." Even "driving" at that speed, they are easy to see.

However, if you want something soothing and serene, stick to cool tones of blue, green, or purple. They send a more relaxing vibe. Even the dramatic spires of purple monkshood and salvia look cool and chic rather than flamboyant, especially if they're strutting their stuff in a purple ceramic vase. Pastels, too, are always tranquil. Even a rainbow of pastel shades makes a beguiling bouquet, because the tints are so soft and gentle. And don't forget about white. It will cool down a display that's too hot or add a fresh sparkle to one that's a bit insipid.

Yet another guideline is to take cues from Mother Nature. Blue, green, and purple seem to "paint" a roiling sea. Magenta, orange, red, and yellow recall the hues of a setting sun. Purple, red, and yellow mimic a meadow, while blue and white evoke a summer sky with puffy clouds. All these color combinations work well in bouquets. There are many more to choose from—just look around.

In this floral foam color wheel there are green nicotiana, hosta leaves, and ivy berries; blue pansies, monkshood, salvia, and ageratum; pink roses and Sheffield mums: red roses and sedum 'Autumn Joy'; and orange zinnias and dahlias with a few ornamental peppers thrown in. Renegade flowers that were blooming out of season, such as yellow St. John's wort and purple bellflower, made it possible to complete the wheel.

INDIVIDUAL COLOR CUES

Every color has its own personality, and through much trial and error, I've learned just how to mix certain ones together and when to keep them apart. I think of it as I would a dinner party: While I appreciate all of my friends, I realize they have very different traits and some don't blend with others.

- **Red electrifies and energizes.** It always draws attention to itself, like an exclamation mark. If mixed in with several different colors, a little red goes a long way, so keep it at a minimum. However, paired with yellow, red seems less exuberant, so I use it with abandon.

- **Pinks can be as hot and sizzling** as flamingos, or softly romantic as in a bouquet of light pink peonies. Pink can be too sweet at times, but a touch of red nearby can liven it up. Blues and purples give pinks a lift, too.

- And, for something truly unexpected, **marry pink with orange;** a deep pink rose, perhaps, with flaming orange trumpet vine.

- **Speaking of orange**, I enjoy it for the sheer fright of its hue: It is a startling color. Even people who like it don't always know how to handle it. A swath of orange dahlias perks up the dullest setting. Combined with fall foliage, they could jump-start a car! Add deep purple monks-hood to the mix to tone it down a notch.

- **Yellow is the first color your eye sees.** It attracts and dominates. Yellow classically combines with blue or purple, its chromatic counterpoint. White and yellow is another traditional combo, clear and refreshing. A touch of orange works well with yellow, too.

- Since most flowers have green foliage, **green is often ignored as a color with pizzazz of its own.** Yet, green is a stabilizer, a calming influence on other colors. Dousing an arrangement of flaming colors with green leaves can make the whole display more harmonious. Many conifers and hostas have blue-green, dark green, or gold-green foliage. Other plants bear leaves in hundreds of shades—lime, emerald, moss, or sometimes green blended with burgundy, purple, or gray. Green flowers, however, are few and far between, but a green and white arrangement is always stunning. Favorite green flowers include the balls of chartreuse viburnum and 'Annabelle' hydrangea, as well as the lime green, frothy sprays of lady's mantle and the disks of 'Envy' zinnia.

- **Pure white can be a cold color,** but most white flowers have hints of another color—pink, yellow, blue—blushing through them. If you can spot these other tints, it's nice to bring them out by arranging them with other flowers of that hue. Or, keep the bouquet all white and notice how many tints of it you can spy. Best of all, white goes with everything and can act as a peacemaker in any bouquet.

Once you have your colors down pat, you're almost there. Step back and take a second look, checking the bouquet for a play of shapes. If everything seems too round, for instance, insert a few spiky flowers—foxglove, monkshood, or salvia. And vice versa; you might need to add rounded shapes to a spiky bouquet.

Orange tree peonies, yellow honeysuckle, and purple dame's rocket make a colorful spring bouquet.

SCENTS AND SENSIBILITY

Adding fragrant flowers to a bouquet makes a big difference in how the bouquet makes you feel. A scented blossom has the power to alter a mood, lift the spirits, and even trigger a long-lost memory. Yet, unlike color or shape, aroma is rarely considered in planning an arrangement. Think how many times you leaned in to sniff a bouquet, only to be disappointed.

Designing with a nose for scent can open up a whole new world of delights. The fragrance creates an intimacy beckoning you closer and insisting you linger. So take time to smell your flowers and include fragrant varieties. It should be noted, however, that a flower's perfume is not always in its petals. Plants convey scent through the medium of essential oils. These essences may be diffused through all of the tissues of the plant: fruit, seed, gum, leaf, petal, root, or stem. Salvia and scented geranium hide their perfume in their foliage. You need to ruffle them or split a leaf to release it. And the strength of the perfume varies enormously from plant to plant. A single lily can perfume a room, while it takes a bunch of roses or daffodils to make their scent known.

THE POWER OF ONE

I've never met a flower that wasn't fetching alone. Each is a marvel of nature's design. Large flowers, such as tree peonies, plate-size dahlias, and overblown roses, are the ultimate solo artists, thanks in great part to their size. But smaller blooms are equally distinctive, especially if placed where they are sure to be seen—a single daisy tucked into a chemistry vial on a night table or a cheery daffodil in a bud vase on the bathroom sink. Such singular perfection becomes oh-so-much-more when individual blooms follow one another down the center of a table or along a windowsill. Don't underestimate the power of repetition.

Remember, too, that fragrance, like taste, is personal and subjective. Those flowers with strong seductive scents—lilies, lilacs, hyacinths, and some daffodils—may be too heady for some people, so use them in moderation and certainly keep them off the dinner table. The tiny fragrant flowers—cowslips, dianthus, snowdrops, and winter aconite—have trouble making their presence known, so place them in spots where people can bend down and take a whiff. A nosegay of these gems on a night table will make waking up more enjoyable and may even scent a guest's dreams. Other flowers hold back until dusk, then grace the evening with their perfume: Hall's honeysuckle, petunias, and *Nicotiana sylvestris* are a few of these twilight charmers.

As you begin adding fragrant blooms to your bouquets, you'll find that they cast a magic spell: The more you have, the more you'll want. But don't worry—each season has its own perfume. As spring's whiffs of daffodils, lilacs, and peonies wane, summer's perfumes of honeysuckle, lilies, and roses blare. The fragrances of fall's sweet autumn clematis, joined by those of moonflowers and pineapple sage, dance on the wind. Winter's subtler scents of balsam, snowdrops, and snow crocus are overpowered by witch hazel. I'll always make room for another sensational scent in the garden—and in a bouquet.

OPPOSITE: One large-flowered clematis blossom in a small vase can steal the show. ABOVE: A wreath of pachysandra is embroidered with roses, honeysuckle, and variegated euonymus.

CONTAINER CHIC

Containers can take an arrangement from so-so to sensational, but a few simple ones will give you a good head start. One reason is that each container changes its look depending on the flowers it holds. Although I have been collecting vases for decades, more often than not I repeatedly use my favorites. These include a simple green pottery jug, a glass celery jar, and an orange pitcher. You'll notice them in many photos throughout this book. And consider this: A simple water glass can be as beautiful as a crystal vase when it holds gorgeous flowers, as all eyes are on the blooms.

But unique and unusual containers have a value all their own. They catch the eye immediately, making a statement that can't be overlooked. Depending on what is used, such vessels can set a mood, carry out a theme, or be just plain funny. Conch shells bring the beach to the table for informal entertaining, while a silver tureen stuffed with white peonies smacks of high-end elegance. Wooden buckets or hollowed-out logs brimming with wildflowers work for a rustic retreat. Rubber boots concealing water glasses that hold the branches of spring-blooming shrubs make a clear statement about spring rains. Gravy boats, eggcups, teapots, tumblers, shot glasses, wine goblets, decanters, and other kitchen staples always look at home on a dining room table. Quirky collectibles such as porcelain hands, cranberry vases, or glass baskets look even better when displaying flowers. In the garden, a wicker plant stand, a hanging basket, a window box, a birdbath, or even a wheelbarrow is arresting when filled with flowers.

There's also the appeal of nature's own bounty. Pumpkins and watermelons are charming when filled with flowers. Watermelons' watery flesh acts like floral foam, and you only need to stick in the flowers. A pumpkin, on the other hand, needs to be hollowed out and fitted with a plastic liner and floral foam, or even quicker, with a bowl of water. The truth is that most anything can become a container whether you use it as is, line it, or stash a waterproof vessel inside.

A POSY IN THE HAND

As I design bouquets, I mix and match flowers in my hand to see what works together. It is child's play and cathartic. For a spur-of-the-moment bouquet, I walk through the garden collecting flowers in my hand as I go. In less than 10 minutes, I have enough to fill a vase.

I start with a few of the same flowers for the center of the bouquet in my left hand, than add another and another, always rotating the bouquet as I go to keep the first group of flowers in the center. Once the posy is complete, I pair it with a vase.

I check the fullness of the bouquet against the opening of the vase to make sure it fits. Too skimpy a bunch won't hold its shape well when it stands in water. Too big a bunch will be squished and damaged when it is forced into the vase. Once the bouquet has the right girth, I hold it next to the vase to roughly measure the length at which to cut the stems. I cut the stems the same length, remove any foliage that would be below the waterline, and put the handful of flowers into the vase.

OPPOSITE AND LEFT: **For this blue, chartreuse, and purple bouquet, I chose blue lupine for the center. The spikes form the peak of the dome. Lady's mantle was added next. Its chartreuse glow lights up the blue lupine. Then Japanese iris and bearded iris were added. They bring a different shape to the bouquet with solid blocks of complementary color. The other flowers—in various shades of purple—add their own distinct looks. Allium 'Purple Sensation' is an airy bloom. Blue columbine repeats the blue of the lupine, but in a small delicate shape. Purple dame's rocket, bearded iris, and catmint give the bouquet a lift with their floral perfumes.**

FLORAL FOAM: BUILDING BLOCK FOR ARRANGEMENTS

The most useful tool in a flower arranger's cupboard is floral foam, an open-celled foam made from a resin. It is used as a base for an arrangement. When a flower stem is inserted into the foam, the foam holds it securely. The foam's structure resembles plant cells, designed to wick up water and hold it. A saturated 3-inch by 4-inch by 9-inch foam brick holds 40 times its dry weight in water, or about 2 quarts. When a stem is inserted an inch or so into the wet foam, it is able to draw up water. The water in the top of the foam is constantly replaced by water from the cells beneath it. The foam must be kept moist for the life of the arrangement. Since the bricks readily absorb water, the water isn't likely to spill out when moving the arrangement around. Floral foam comes in various shapes, such as balls, blocks,

OPPOSITE AND BELOW: A wooden swan is outfitted with a block of floral foam in a plastic container before the golden Hakone grass and blue lupine are poked in.

bricks, cones, cylinders, spheres, and wreaths, and in an assortment of colors from yellow and pink to blue and green. Floral foam bricks are also available caged in plastic with a handle on each side and can be used to hang flowers on an arch, a church pew, a garden bench, or a railing (see page 135). Mini-Deco holders are domes of floral foam, 2 inches in diameter, glued to plastic bases. The Mini-Deco holders are backed by peel-and-stick adhesive and can be affixed to a wrapped package, the front of a wine bottle, or the top of a candlestick (see page 143). You'll find that the only limitations with floral foam are with your imagination. Since I don't want the under-pinnings of an arrangement to show or distract from the flowers, I buy green. (Oasis is the trade-mark and a commonly used name for the most widely used floral foam products.)

Bricks are the most useful shape and come in sizes that are easily cut with a sharp knife into any shape to fit baskets, birdbaths, bowls, candle cups, containers, seashells, and vases—you name it. The bottom of each brick is pricked with tiny holes to help it absorb water. Once you cut the brick into the shape needed, free-float it, bottom side down, in a bucket of water mixed with the proper amount of floral preservative. (Just follow the directions on the box of preservative.) Using a preservative helps to ensure that cut flowers stay fresh as long as possible. As water is absorbed into the brick, it will begin to sink and turn a darker green. Never force the brick underwater. Doing so traps air inside the brick and reduces your flowers' ability to absorb water. The brick is completely soaked when only a $\frac{1}{4}$ inch of foam floats above the surface of the water.

Happily, this whole saturation process takes less than a minute.

Floral foam can be placed in a bowl or any other waterproof container. If the arrangement is in a basket, a plastic liner is necessary. A deli food container or a plastic food storage box works as a liner as long as it fits tightly in the container. Floral suppliers and craft stores sell baskets with matching liners. Once the floral foam is placed in the container, it is taped in place with floral waterproof tape.

If a stiff flower or foliage stem is cut on a slant, the point can be easily and

smoothly poked into the foam. The end of the stem must be inserted deep enough to be held in place but it should not come out the other side. Some flower stems are too soft to poke into foam; colchicum, crocus, and pansies are soft-stemmed flowers. Some flower stems may split or bend at the bottom when they're poked into foam. Hyacinths are an example. To keep them from splitting or bending, I circle the bottom of each stem with tape before I poke it into the foam; the tape helps to support it.

If a container is to be seen from all sides, I place the tallest stems in the middle, then work my way around with shorter stems until it is full. Nodding and drooping blooms are placed around the edge to blur the line between the container and the bouquet. If the container is only viewed from the front, the tallest stems go at the back and sides, shaping the bouquet. Shorter stems in descending order are positioned from the middle to the front.

OPPOSITE AND ABOVE: A basket with a plastic liner can hold bricks of floral foam. The foam is taped in place before the assorted English roses are added.

My wooden swan cries out for tail feathers. Outfitted with floral foam in a low-sided, plastic liner, I added golden Hakone grass to imitate the look of tail feathers and spiky lupine plumes for a swan longing to be a peacock. Another time, I started with a base of Hall's honeysuckle and poked in St. John's wort, yarrow, and coreopsis. The same dish can have many different looks, depending on the season.

WREATHING THE SEASONS

Wreaths are so versatile, the possibilities so limitless. I ring in every season welcoming guests with wreaths on the garden gate or the front door. Wreaths also make delightful centerpieces: Set on a table, the circles of bloom surround candles of all kinds—a plump pillar, a single slim taper, a candelabra, a lantern, or several small votives, depending on the occasion. In a draft, I surround the candle or candles with a glass chimney to protect them from being blown out by a breeze.

For special occasions, I've added ribbons or copper wires to a large wreath and hung it as a chandelier over a table. If I use a floral foam base, I can poke in some candles for romantic lighting.

For a bit of whimsy, I circle the necks of garden ornaments with blooms. If a floral foam wreath fits over its head, I use that as a base. Otherwise, I make a garland and hang it like a necklace (see page 187). In the winter, I get my kicks dressing up a container of ornamental grass by surrounding it with a conifer wreath. Instead of looking lifeless and dull, the tan grass takes on new life surrounded by green and gold conifers, and its plumes sparkle with snow. Our cement birdbath looks cozy warmed by a fir shawl (see page 151).

OPPOSITE: Metal geese wear floral foam wreaths of flowers. One has pink roses, lilacs, and clematis; another sports 'Gold Star' dogwood; and the third has a mixture of blue iris, chartreuse lady's mantle and ageratum. BELOW: A wreath of peonies, roses, and honeysuckle backed by pachysandra.

There are two different approaches—a wet one and a dry one—to making a wreath. A wet wreath is made on the base of a floral foam ring, which holds water and keeps flowers and foliage fresh for days. A dry wreath form is usually shaped of straw, grapevine, wood, or metal and embellished with dried plants or freshly clipped foliage. Kept outdoors in cool weather, both wet and dry wreaths can last for weeks.

A WET WREATH

I keep a selection of floral foam rings handy for quick and easy decorating for entertaining. Floral rings (Oasis brand ring holders) are available in craft shops, online, or from florists in a range of sizes from 6 to 24 inches in diameter. They are simple to assemble, whether completely covered with the blooms of a single plant (such as roses or hydrangea) when flowers are plentiful or "slipcovered" with an assortment of flowers. When flowers are few, the wreath can be hidden under a collection of foliage with a few flowers poked in for color. The flowers stand out as individuals silhouetted against the foliage. Covered with both the foliage and flowers of rhododendrons or dogwood, a wreath can be made in 10 minutes, once the flowers are collected.

Actually, any small broadleaf foliage, such as ivy, rhododendron, boxwood, Japanese andromeda (*Pieris japonica*), and scented geranium, work to hide the base and draw attention to the blooms. A mix of assorted foliage woven together into a tapestry of textures is a winter favorite.

I often use pachysandra, the most common groundcover in America, as my background. It stays fresh for 3 weeks covering a floral foam wreath if the wreath is kept moist. The flowers adorning the wreath need to be changed several times to keep up. Smoke bush, ivy, fall foliage, inkberry, nandina, conifers, and holly can all be used, too, as background or alone, and easily last 2 weeks.

OPPOSITE: Rings of floral foam in all sizes waiting to be covered. A pachysandra-covered wreath waits for flowers. ABOVE: Cutting the top whorl of pachysandra.

The good thing about pachysandra foliage is that it grows in whorls a few inches apart along the stem. If the top whorl is removed, another one or two remain below and the garden bed doesn't look like it has been plucked. I cut it year 'round,

even if I have to shovel off snow. Once the stems thaw, they thank me for their short indoor vacation.

Each ring of floral foam is mounted on a sturdy, lightweight plastic tray, making it easy to handle. (When using the ring on a table, protect the table from moisture by placing a plate or a placemat underneath it.) Saturate the ring by free-floating it, foam side down, in water mixed with a floral preservative.

Cut foliage and flower stems short, an inch or two, on a sharp angle so they insert easily into the foam without breaking. Poke the stems into the middle of the foam where they can take up water, not out the other side or touching the plastic. Completely cover the form with foliage so no foam or plastic shows before embellishing it with flowers.

OPPOSITE: Covering a wreath with azalea flowers is quick and easy. BELOW: A wreath of dogwood foliage and flowers hanging over a table has candles poked in.

To hang a dogwood wreath as a chandelier, cut three 42-inch lengths of copper

wire. Equally space and attach the wires to the floral foam circle by wrapping one end of each around it and twisting it in place. Connect the three loose ends together by twisting them securely above the middle of the circle. Gently push equally spaced candles into the foam until they rest on the plastic base. Then completely cover the wreath with individual sprigs of dogwood. I used Kousa dogwood 'Summer Stars' flowers and foliage. This cultivar holds its flowers for 2 months or more on the tree and a week in a wreath. Once complete, the wreath can be hung from a ceiling hook or the branch of a tree. To keep the foam moist and the flowers fresh, set the wreath in a sink of water or spritz it as needed, usually every day or two.

A DRY WREATH

In fall and winter, I make dry wreaths that
will last without water. The base of a dry
wreath can be straw, grapevine, wood, or
metal and can be reused because it's
long lasting.

I decorate grapevine wreaths by poking
sprigs of berries, fall foliage, dried flowers,
and seed heads between the twisted vines.
If needed, I secure clippings or objects like
bird's nests or pinecones with 24-gauge
green floral wire.

A straw wreath is held together with clear
plastic fishing line. I poke twigs with multiple oak leaves into the straw and under
the fishing line, making sure all stems
point the same way around the circle. Berries can be held in place by poking hair-
pins into the straw (see page 108).

It is often surprising how long the dry wreaths keep, flaunting their beauty
in stormy weather. A grapevine wreath decorated with bittersweet, oak
leaves, and artificial birds (see page 115) stayed on the entrance gate for a
month. It kept its good looks after numerous downpours and windy days. A
straw wreath hung on the peak of the porch roof braved the elements for
almost 2 months. It was covered in oak leaves, bittersweet, and Linden
viburnum berries (*Viburnum dilatatum*) with a lotus pod as an accent. It's a
fact: Mother Nature's designs last.

Square wreaths stand out simply by being a different shape. I use wire forms and old wooden picture frames for bases. In fall, I cover frames with bunches of leaves and rose hips. Individual bunches of five to six branches of oak or maple leaves mixed with two or three stems of rose hips are taped or wired together. After securing the end of a 24-gauge floral wire (which comes on a flat paddle) to the wreath form, I wind the wire around and around it as each bundle is added. The wire is easier to work with if it is unwound straight from its paddle, rather than cut off in lengths. The wire holds each bundle securely in place, yet is thin enough that it doesn't show. As I work around the frame, I point all of the stems in the same direction; each bundle of stems is hidden as the foliage of the next group is added. To make it more interesting, one fall I poked in clusters of red, green, and yellow cherry tomatoes that were left hanging on the vine. It was late in the season, and they

OPPOSITE AND ABOVE: A square wreath made on a wooden form has the stems of maple leaves, berries, and rose hips secured as the paddle of wire is wound around them.

had been nipped by frost, so they had lost their flavor.

Round metal frames come in an assortment of sizes. The traditional way to decorate them is with evergreens, each bunch wired in place and overlapping the next bunch as I move around the frame. Even though they are simple to make, I prefer to purchase ready-made plain wreaths of Fraser fir and then customize them with conifers from my garden. Metal wreaths in other shapes, such as squares, stars, and trees, are decorated using the same techniques (see page 133).

MOCK TOPIARIES

Mock topiaries can be formal or casual, depending on the flowers and foliage used. They can be made in any size with a ball of flowers on a single trunk or with multiple puffs of flowers at the top of a branching trunk. It might suit your purpose to shape tight balls of flowers in a "poodle cut," or to relax the branch of flowers for a "shaggy dog" look with strands of long elegant vines gracefully draping down. All have their time and place.

OPPOSITE: A large topiary with roses, ivy, and more grouped in tight balls like a "poodle cut." BELOW: A relaxed "shaggy dog" style topiary made with variegated ivy, dahlias, Jerusalem artichoke, zinnias, and more.

I collect interesting branches for just this purpose. Some are cut from the trees and vines in my garden, others are branches that have blown down. Those with patterned bark, such as white birch, river birch, golden birch, London plane tree (*Platanus*), and coral-bark maple (*Acer Palmatum* 'Sango Kaku'), make the most interesting trunks for topiaries. Sometimes a twisted hardwood vine, such as a wisteria, works as a base, too.

The ideal look of the finished topiary is tall and lean, not short and squat, although the bottom container can be short and squat to provide stability to the top. Create a small tabletop topiary by inserting a 3-foot-long straight branch, an inch or two in diameter, into a 6-inch plastic pot or a pint deli food container filled with wet plaster of paris. Plaster of paris dries quickly and is heavy enough to anchor the flowers and foliage that are placed on the top. Be sure the plastic container fits snugly inside another more decorative pot.

When the plaster hardens, push a cube of moistened floral foam onto the tip of the branch, mold chicken wire around the foam, and secure it to the branch with green floral tape or wire. The foam should be smaller than the potted base by several inches, because once the flowers are added to it, the diameter will increase by 4 to 6 inches.

Cut the stems of the flowers short and poke them into the corners and sides of the foam, turning the cube into a ball. As you work, keep turning the topiary to make it balanced. Flowers and foliage are heavy. If you finish the front without adding flowers to the back, it might topple.

A multiple-branching topiary is constructed following the same instructions. The taller the form and the more branches, the more important it is to make the topiary balanced, preventing the structure from toppling in the wind. Ideally, the top of the topiary should be as big around as the base, but with larger branching topiaries, that is not possible—it would look too clunky. An elegant long line is the ideal. It is helpful to put the base into a much larger pot instead, then stabilize it with a weight such as a large rock or two in the bottom.

Topiary forms can be saved and reused once the flowers fade. New foam should be added before inserting fresh greens and flowers for the next party.

BELOW: To make a mock topiary, mix plaster of paris with water in a deli container. OPPOSITE: Next, add a decorative stick and let the plaster harden. Put the form in a decorative pot and hide the plaster with moss. Place a cube of floral foam on top of the stick, surround it with chicken wire, and add flowers.

Another, simpler, idea for making a mock topiary is to poke a 2- to 3-foot pointed branch securely into the middle of a pot of a low-growing plant, preferably a draping plant such as ivy. Potted ivy doesn't mind being poked. If the stick is poked in 6 inches or more, the soil holds it in place. Follow the directions above for adding a cube of floral foam to the top of the stick and decorating it with flowers.

On another occasion, after a live azalea topiary died, I clipped off the top branches and used the stem and roots as a topiary form by outfitting it with a fresh globe of flowers. Even though the roots were dead, they had a firm grasp of the soil and held the stem in place for years—another amazing garden feat!

CANDLE CUPS

If space is limited on the dining table or mantle, a candlestick with a cluster of flowers surrounding the candle is ideal. The floral arrangement is moved up off the table and placed where it is more easily seen surrounding the candle. Candle cups are the floral device designed for this purpose. Each cup is shaped to hold a small scoop of floral foam. The knob on the bottom of the cup snugly fits into the top of most candlesticks. A candle is pushed into the top of the foam and flowers are poked in around it. The floral arrangement is eye-catching, balanced on top of a candlestick pedestal. You can soften the look by trailing a vine, such as small-leaved ivy, honeysuckle, or clematis, from a tall candlestick.

You can create numerous looks with candle cups depending on your choice of candlesticks and flowers. Set a casual table with a pair of rustic wooden candlesticks or create an elegant look with a single candlestick in china, silver, or crystal. Candle cups may be used to dress up a large branching candelabra as well. Place a candle cup of flowers in the center, so that it's surrounded by arms holding candles.

To create a candle cup arrangement, first outfit the candle cup with floral foam. Visualize the shape by thinking of a scoop of ice cream fitting into its cone. With a

sharp knife, I carve a scoop out of a brick of floral foam, but balls of foam are also available if you prefer to skip the carving step.

Float the foam in water until it is dark green and completely saturated. It takes less than a minute. Next, secure the foam to the cup with floral tape before placing the cup's knob into the candlestick. If the cup wobbles in the candleholder, a piece of floral clay can be pushed into the hole. Like gum, clay holds it in place. If a candle is to be added, I place it into the top of the floral foam before adding the flowers and greens. The candle can be poked directly into the foam or into a plastic candleholder with a pointed base that is poked into the foam. Sometimes it's festive to have flowers without the candle.

When roses are plentiful in early summer, I cover the foam completely with flowers. For this candle cup, I chose an assortment of yellow and orange roses in different sizes and also poked in honeysuckle to add a differently shaped flower.

If flowers are few, it is best to cover the floral foam first with greens (pachysandra works year 'round) and trailing plants, such as ivy, to hide the foam before adding the flowers. The arrangement won't look skimpy and each flower will be noticed. In winter, a combination of colorful evergreens is beautiful for its own sake; no flowers are needed.

FROM FAR LEFT TO RIGHT: Cut floral foam to fit a candle cup. Shape it into a globe and tape it in place atop a candlestick. Add a candle in a plastic candleholder, if desired. Then add the roses and honeysuckle.

GARLANDS

Garlands are so simple to make and versatile that I hope more people will give them a try. A garland is a way to make a big statement with ease. Nothing could be simpler. Larger garlands can wind around a railing, frame a door, edge a table, and drape across a mantle. Smaller ones make glorious headbands, hatbands, napkin rings, and dog collars.

The most common garlands are made with a ribbon, a rope, or a vine such as honeysuckle or ivy as their base. Individual flowers and groups of flowers are attached by twisting small-gauge picture or floral wire around them. For a smaller garland, the wire is twisted around individual flower stems to attach them to a ribbon. A larger garland uses a rope or length of vine as a base. The flowers and foliage are first wired into groups of six or eight

After soaking the floral foam garland for a minute or so until it was filled with water, I covered it in 3- to 4-inch pieces of mock orange. To finish it, I poked in assorted roses including 'Belinda', a rose with clusters of single flowers, and the deep purple rose 'Reine des Violettes'.

stems; then the groups are wired to the rope or vine. When making either a small or large garland, start at one end and move along the ribbon, rope, or vine, attaching flowers with their stems pointing in the same direction. Each flower or group of flowers you add should overlap with the group that preceded it.

J. Barry Ferguson, a renowned florist, taught me to wire roses around a ribbon. Teddy, my West Highland terrier, wore one to my daughter Margaret's wedding. A ribbon wired with roses doubles as a child's headband or as a lady's hatband. If conditioned, rosebuds and newly opened roses last for a day or more out of water.

OPPOSITE, CLOCKWISE FROM TOP RIGHT: I'm wearing a headband of roses, lilacs, and dame's rocket wired onto a ribbon. Spanish bluebells and clematis are strung on dental floss for a rabbit's necklace. My son Tom holds our dog in his floral collar at my daughter's wedding. A garland of greens had peonies and roses in water picks poked in after it was hung up.

A newer invention is an Oasis floral foam garland made of cylinders of foam, like sausage links encased in green netting. The garlands come in 9- or 32.8-foot lengths, but can be cut to any size between the links. Soak the foam in water before it is covered with greens and flowers. The moist foam keeps the garland fresh longer. It can be made a day ahead, kept in a cool spot, and hung up the day of the party. The netting makes it easy to attach along the back of a garden bench, along a railing, or over an arbor, window, or door.

A Hawaiian-style lei is a garland of another sort. The flowers last only a day or so, but the memory of having a lei draped around your neck can last a lifetime. For modern leis, flowers are strung together using a long needle and dental floss. A lei needle can be from 6 to 12 inches long. The flowers are strung along the floss to whatever length is needed. They can be made a day ahead and kept in a refrigerator. I have found many uses for leis—placed around the neck of a guest of honor or a garden ornament, adorning straw hats, and swagged around birdbaths and buffet tables. In other words, leis can be featured in many of the same places where other garlands are used.

Coaxing a Bud
to Open

As much as I love buds in bouquets, there are times when I'd prefer an open flower. Once they are fully developed, many swollen buds relax and open with a little massaging. I've done it with alliums, peonies, and poppies. It is worth a shot with any cup-shaped flower. The trick is to be gentle and not to force or rip the petals.

To unfurl a tight bud, dunk it in warm water a few times, bend back the surrounding green sepals, and massage or squeeze the bud gently on several sides where the bud meets the stem. Run your hand lightly over the top to help it start to unfurl. If it does not completely open immediately, it will continue to open over the course of the day.

OPPOSITE: Bending back the sepals of a poppy and gently squeezing its base helps it relax and open. LEFT: A peony can be massaged to open.

WRAPPING IT UP

I've never met a person who didn't appreciate a gift of flowers. So a posy topping a gift-wrapped package holds the promise of unstoppable smiles and barely controlled giddiness: It is the equivalent of giving two gifts in one.

I wrap my packages with a plain color or small-print paper so the focus is on my flowers instead. A nosegay of freshly cut and conditioned flowers easily lasts for hours out of water. I secure the posy first with a rubber band, then tie a ribbon around it, hiding the band. The posy can be tied to the package with a ribbon or held in place with clear tape at the last minute. If the recipient puts it into water, it will go merrily along for days. Remember, flowers sold in the wholesale market are often out of water for a day or more.

Grasses and liriope can be tied around a package like a ribbon. Leaves of inkberry or euonymus can be glued onto the paper in patterns. There are many creative variations on the same idea. Foliage lasts for days, sometimes weeks. Obviously, a bouquet of dried flowers—lavender and salvia or seedpods such as money plant and rose hips—lasts for months.

For a long-lasting fresh flower arrangement, I use a floral foam bouquet holder, the kind that brides carry. Although fancy silver- or gold-handled models are available, an inexpensive one with a plastic handle usually suits my purposes. I poke flowers and foliage into the moist floral foam, circling the form and filling each opening so the handle never shows. The handle is then taped to the package. The receiver can lay the arrangement on a table as a centerpiece.

PROLONGING THE BLOOM

The most important step for prolonging the life of cut flowers and foliage is conditioning them before arranging. *Conditioning* is a catchall term used by professionals describing the series of steps taken to extend the life of cut flowers for maximum enjoyment. There are general guidelines that work for most flowers, but alas, flowers, like people, are individuals. Each flower has a different life expectancy. A few quirky ones take exception to the general methods of conditioning, requiring a few twists of their own. Individual flowers' needs are listed in "The Vase Life of Garden Flowers" on page 198.

Allan M. Armitage conducted extensive tests on a long list of flowers to discover the earliest that a flower can be picked without damaging its ability to open. "Generally, professionals harvest 'in the bud' as flowers begin to show color, because it reduces the space [needed] during shipping and there is less damage to buds than [to] open flowers," says Armitage. "Home gardeners, too, can pick at the bud stage for the longest vase life." However, there are exceptions. Some spikelike flowers, such as monkshood and delphiniums, should have at least a few flowers fully open on the stem prior to harvest. Flowers of the aster family, the largest family of flowering plants (including daisies, eupatorium, and yarrow), require their blooms to be open and pollen visible before they're picked. If picked closed, they won't open.

There are other variables besides conditioning and harvest time that affect the length of time a flower lasts in a bouquet. If a bloom is poked into floral foam instead of plunked into water, its life is shorter by a day or two. Also, the shorter the stem, the longer the vase life, especially with roses. A shorter stem allows water to reach the bloom quickly and easily.

If flowers are kept in a cool rather than warm room, they last longer. Sitting on a sunny windowsill shortens their life. Their water evaporates faster, too. Always keep the water in the vase or floral foam topped up. After a few days in the vase, a change of water adds days to the life of the bouquet.

On flowers with layered petals, such as dahlias and roses, the outer petals usually brown first while the inner ones retain their freshness. By removing the brown petals, you can extend the flowers' vase life by a few more days. Spiky flowers, such as foxglove, lupine, campanula, and monkshood, have flowers that open in succession along their stems. As the older blooms droop, they can be removed to leave the newer ones to brighten the vase. On flowers with several blooms extending out from a central stem, such as fool's onion and agapanthus, remove the oldest blooms as they droop. The younger, fresher ones will carry the show. Believe it or not, it is possible to keep some freshly snipped blooms, such as large-flowered clematis and blue salvia, around for 2 weeks or more—long enough to need dusting!

Freshly cut garden
flowers waiting to be
conditioned include roses,
salvia, alliums, peonies,
bachelor's buttons,
dogwood, love-in-a-mist,
and lupine.

MYTH: Placing flowers up to their necks in water increases their uptake.

FACT: Relatively little water is absorbed through the stems of most flowers, although violets, I'm told, can take in water through their petals. The only advantage in having 6 inches rather than 1 inch of water in a vase is that the increased water pressure will force the water to rise 6 inches up the water-conducting tissues of the stem, reducing the height the water must be moved by the flower's own capillary action.

MYTH: Many florists recommend recutting stems underwater to prevent air bubbles from clogging them. Air bubbles prevent stems from taking up water.

FACT: Recutting stems underwater is an awkward feat at best in a bucket and impossible in a narrow vase. A contortionist comes to mind. In Dr. Armitage's tests, it didn't make a significant difference, and for most of us, it is not worth the time or effort. However, recutting flower stems at an angle just before placing them into water or floral foam increases the stems' surface area for taking up water and eliminates air bubbles that may have formed if the flowers were left lying in the air too long.

MYTH: Hammering the cut ends of woody stems from trees and shrubs allows more water to flow up them.

FACT: Woody stems should never be hammered. Hammering causes damage to the tissues and shortens the branches' life. Instead, splitting the stem ends with a sharp knife or pruners half an inch up from the bottom increases their uptake of water.

MYTH: Recutting the stems of flowers every few days lengthens their life.

FACT: If rose and stock (*Matthiola*) stems are recut every few days, they do last longer. But recutting the stems of most flowers makes no difference in how long they last. However, cutting does shorten the stems, allowing easier movement of water to the flowers. In fact, the shorter the distance needed for water to travel, the easier it is to get to the flower. So if a flower head comes loose from its stem, float it in water, and you can enjoy looking into its face. Flowers do often last longer this way.

A candle cup fitted into the middle of a candelabra holds dahlias, cup and saucer vine, and clematis seed heads.

DURABLE FOLIAGE

Generally, foliage lasts longer than flowers in arrangements and often dries naturally, adding weeks to your display. 'Wood's Dwarf' nandina is a good example. Many other leaves—hosta and ivy for instance—can be laid on a table to make a "runner" and look fresh for days out of water. However, new spring growth in its first flush of green is too soft and usually does not last long.

GUIDELINES FOR CONDITIONING FLOWERS

1. KEEP IT CLEAN. Clean buckets, pruners, and water cut down on bacteria that plug stems and cause rotting. If placed in a "bacterial stew," flowers die of thirst; the microbes plug stem ends, preventing water from flowing up them. It is floral murder. A solution of a few drops of liquid dishwashing soap and a teaspoon of bleach per gallon of water destroys bacteria.

2. HARVEST BLOOMS EARLY. The right times to pick are first thing in the morning after the dew has dried, or in the evening after the sun is low and the air has cooled. The advantage to picking in the morning is that the stems are turgid and filled with moisture, and the flowers are less likely to wilt. In the evening, the flowers are packed with carbohydrates from a day of photosynthesizing, and carbohydrates prolong their life in the vase. However, the flowers have sufficient carbohydrates in the morning, and that combined with their turgidity—especially on hot days—makes morning the best time to pick them.

Use clean, sharp pruners, not scissors, to cut the flowers. Scissors squeeze and crush stems. Don't break off stems, either. Flowers picked as soon as they open and before their pollen appears last the longest. Once a lot of pollen appears on the petals, the flower is senescing; a senescing flower is rapidly aging and will have a short vase life. As with all generalizations, there are exceptions. Yarrow, if cut before its pollen appears, wilts. For individual flower requirements, check "The Vase Life of Garden Flowers" on page 198.

3. CLIP EXCESS FOLIAGE. All foliage that would be below the waterline in a vase should be removed to prevent decay. Decay smells bad and hastens the decline of the flowers.

4. CONDITION CUT FLOWERS. Cut flower stems on an angle and set them in a clean bucket of warm water with a floral preservative mixed in. Refrigerate the flowers or place them in a cool place, a basement, or a dark corner of an air-conditioned room for 6 hours or overnight before arranging them. The life of most cut flowers more than triples when they are held at 40°F for at least 6 hours before they are arranged. Cool air temperatures are the number one factor in extending a flower's life. This is how growers condition flowers for their dry flights to floral markets around the world.

OPPOSITE: Hot water restores turgidity in wilted stems. ABOVE: Some flowers such as clematis and love-in-a-mist last longer if their stems are sealed with a flame.

However, there are exceptions to the warm-water bath: Astilbe plumes will last longer—12 days rather than 2 to 4—if placed in hot water first, allowed to cool down, and then refrigerated.

Adding a floral preservative to the water is essential for prolonging the life of most flowers. A preservative both stops bacteria from growing and feeds the flowers. "Studies have shown that floral preservative can increase vase life up to 75 percent," says Armitage. Sweetly scented pincushion flowers (*Scabiosa atropurpurea*) last from 5 to 7 days in plain water; using a preservative adds 3 to 5 more days. And the days are more than doubled for gooseneck loosestrife (*Lysimachia clethroides*), from 5 to 12.

Blooms from bulbs and rhizomes, as well as flowers with hollow stems, don't

benefit from preservatives' nutrients. Actually, large-flowered clematis, euphorbia, poppies, and other flowers that ooze a milky sap called latex when they are cut need to have their stem ends sealed over a flame. Otherwise, their sap runs out, and they droop and wilt. The sap is messy, and in some cases, can be an irritant if it comes in contact with your skin.

5. PERK THEM UP. Warm water resuscitates wilted flowers. However, for restoring turgidity in wilted stems, hot water (110°F) is recommended. For woody or badly wilted stems, very hot water (180°F to 200°F) is better. Place the stems in an inch of hot water for only 30 seconds. Wrap the flower heads in newspaper to protect them from the steam of the hot water. The flowers should revive in 15 to 30 minutes. Then recut their stems and put them in cool water in a refrigerator or in a cool place for a few hours.

WATER QUALITY

Most of us don't question the quality of the water that comes out of our taps when we are using it for flower arrangements, but water quality does affect the vase life of flowers. If your tap water is "hard," it probably contains calcium carbonate and calcium sulfate and may occasionally contain high concentrations of magnesium. If your tap water is "soft," it has high concentrations of sodium ions. Both extremes are bad for floral life. The same is true of fluoridated water.

If your flowers don't hold up as long as you think they should, have your water tested. Your county extension agent can do this or direct you to the proper labs. If you discover that your tap water may be decreasing the vase life of your flowers, you can use purified or bottled water instead.

THE VASE LIFE OF GARDEN FLOWERS

This section is a guide to help you plan ahead when cutting and arranging flowers for special occasions. It provides the approximate number of days that a newly cut and conditioned flower can be expected to live in an arrangement if picked at the appropriate time, conditioned, and kept in water. Knowing when to cut flowers and knowing their probable vase life has many advantages. It permits planning ahead and arranging flowers without worrying that they might not look fresh when needed. It can influence decisions on which flowers to plant for cutting and how to condition them to last a week or more (especially when you're taking a bouquet to a friend). It is surprising how long many of them last.

My studies of the vase life of flowers are not as scientific as those of Allan Armitage: I couldn't control room temperatures nor the moisture in the air. And it wasn't always possible for me to know the exact day a flower opened. But, actually, my experiences may be closer to what you might also experience. In real-life situations, we can't always control the temperature or the humidity.

Freshly picked flowers— lilacs, lily-of-the-valley, pink dogwood, tree peonies, 'Queen of the Night' tulips, parrot tulips, and bluebells—are each placed in their own vase and set in the garden house to see how long they last in water.

Achillea 'Coronation Gold'
Coronation gold yarrow
FLOWER COLOR: Yellow
BLOOM TIME: Summer
FRAGRANCE: Pungent herbal
WHEN TO HARVEST: When the flower is open and pollen is visible
SPECIAL NEEDS: Hang stems upside down to dry for winter bouquets.
VASE LIFE: 7 to 12 days

A. filipendulina
Yarrow
FLOWER COLOR: Gold
BLOOM TIME: Summer
FRAGRANCE: Pungent herbal
WHEN TO HARVEST: When the flower is open and pollen is visible
SPECIAL NEEDS: Hang stems upside down to dry for winter bouquets.
VASE LIFE: 7 to 12 days

Aconitum sp.
Monkshood, wolf's bane
FLOWER COLOR: Bright blue
BLOOM TIME: Late summer through late fall
FRAGRANCE: None
WHEN TO HARVEST: When the top two or three blooms are open
SPECIAL NEEDS: All parts of this plant are poisonous, so do not expose any cuts or scratches on your hands to its sap. Wearing gloves is advised.
VASE LIFE: 7 to 10 days

Monkshood

Actaea sp.
Baneberry, bugbane, snakeroot
FLOWER COLOR: White
BLOOM TIME: *A. racemosa* blooms from July through August; *A. simplex* 'White Pearl' blooms late September through all of October.
FRAGRANCE: Yes
WHEN TO HARVEST: When half the flowers are open along the stem
SPECIAL NEEDS: None
VASE LIFE: 7 to 10 days

Ageratum houstonianum
Ageratum, floss flower
FLOWER COLOR: White, pinks, blues, and purples
BLOOM TIME: Summer through fall
FRAGRANCE: None
WHEN TO HARVEST: As soon as it opens
SPECIAL NEEDS: None
VASE LIFE: 7 to 10 days

Alchemilla mollis
Lady's mantle
FLOWER COLOR: Chartreuse
BLOOM TIME: June and July
FRAGRANCE: None
WHEN TO HARVEST: When the clusters of tiny flowers are fully open
SPECIAL NEEDS: None
VASE LIFE: 7 to 10 days

Allium aflatunense 'Purple Sensation'
Ornamental onion
FLOWER COLOR: Purple
BLOOM TIME: Summer
FRAGRANCE: None
WHEN TO HARVEST: For fresh arrangements, harvest when half the flowers on the stem open; for dried arrangements, collect the dried flower heads.
SPECIAL NEEDS: None
VASE LIFE: 10 to 14 days

Allium sphaerocephalon
Drumstick allium
FLOWER COLOR: Rosy
BLOOM TIME: Summer
FRAGRANCE: None
WHEN TO HARVEST: When the bottom three or four whorls of flowers open
SPECIAL NEEDS: None
VASE LIFE: 10 to 14 days

Anemone x hybrida
Japanese anemone
FLOWER COLOR: White, pink, and warm rose
BLOOM TIME: Late summer and fall
FRAGRANCE: None
WHEN TO HARVEST: When the flower is open
SPECIAL NEEDS: None
VASE LIFE: 5 to 8 days

Angelonia angustifolia
Angelonia
FLOWER COLOR: Blue and purple
BLOOM TIME: Early summer until killing frost
FRAGRANCE: None
WHEN TO HARVEST: When the first two or three flowers open
SPECIAL NEEDS: None
VASE LIFE: 10 to 14 days

Antirrhinum majus
Snapdragon
FLOWER COLOR: Red, yellow, orange, pink, and white
BLOOM TIME: Summer
FRAGRANCE: None
WHEN TO HARVEST: When a third or a half of the flowers on the stem are open
SPECIAL NEEDS: Highly sensitive to ethylene, a gas given off by ripening fruit. Do not refrigerate near fruit.
VASE LIFE: 5 to 8 days

Aquilegia
Columbine
FLOWER COLOR: Pink, red, white, and blue
BLOOM TIME: Spring
FRAGRANCE: None
WHEN TO HARVEST: When more than half the flowers are open
SPECIAL NEEDS: None
VASE LIFE: 5 to 7 days

Aster novae-angliae
New England aster (assorted cvs. available)
FLOWER COLOR: Blue
BLOOM TIME: Fall
FRAGRANCE: None
WHEN TO HARVEST: As outer petals begin to open
SPECIAL NEEDS: Strip foliage off stems upon harvest.
VASE LIFE: 5 to 7 days

Columbine

Aster novi-belgii
New York aster

FLOWER COLOR: Blue, although cultivars are available in white, red, and pink

BLOOM TIME: Fall

FRAGRANCE: None

WHEN TO HARVEST: As the outer petals begin to open

SPECIAL NEEDS: Strip foliage off stems upon harvest.

VASE LIFE: 8 to 12 days

Astilbe cvs.
Astilbe, false spirea

FLOWER COLOR: Cultivars are available in pink, red, white, and lavender.

BLOOM TIME: Early summer

FRAGRANCE: Most are not fragrant; 'Peach Blossom', a pink cultivar, has a sweet scent.

WHEN TO HARVEST: When two-thirds of the flowers on the stalk are open

SPECIAL NEEDS: Place in hot water (130°F) immediately upon cutting; allow to cool and transfer to water containing floral preservative.

VASE LIFE: 10 to 12 days

Astrantia major
Masterwort

FLOWER COLOR: Pink and white

BLOOM TIME: Early summer

FRAGRANCE: None

WHEN TO HARVEST: When the upper flowers are open

SPECIAL NEEDS: Immediately put in water.

VASE LIFE: 5 to 7 days

Sheffield mum

Baptisia australis
False indigo, blue indigo, wild indigo

FLOWER COLOR: Violet blue

BLOOM TIME: Spring

FRAGRANCE: None

WHEN TO HARVEST: When a third of the flowers are open

SPECIAL NEEDS: Condition immediately in warm water.

VASE LIFE: 7 to 10 days

Buddleja davidii
Butterfly bush, summer lilac

FLOWER COLOR: Blue, white, purple, and yellow

BLOOM TIME: Summer into fall

FRAGRANCE: Baby powder sweet

WHEN TO HARVEST: When half of the flowering spike is open

SPECIAL NEEDS: Condition in warm water (80F° to 100F°) immediately.

VASE LIFE: 5 to 8 days

Camassia leichtlinii
Quamash

FLOWER COLOR: White, cream, blue, and purple

BLOOM TIME: Spring

FRAGRANCE: None

WHEN TO HARVEST: When two or three flowers are open

SPECIAL NEEDS: None

VASE LIFE: 3 to 5 days

Campanula sp.
Bellflower

FLOWER COLOR: White, lavender, and blue

BLOOM TIME: Spring

FRAGRANCE: None

WHEN TO HARVEST: When one or two flowers on the stem are open

SPECIAL NEEDS: Susceptible to ethylene, a gas given off by ripening fruit. Do not refrigerate near fruit.

VASE LIFE: 5 to 8 days

Celosia argentea var. cristata
Cockscomb

FLOWER COLOR: Crimson, scarlet, and gold

BLOOM TIME: Summer through fall

FRAGRANCE: None

WHEN TO HARVEST: When the crested flower is completely open

SPECIAL NEEDS: Strip off the leaves; cockscomb is easily air dried.

VASE LIFE: 7 to 16 days

Centaurea cyanus
Bachelor's button

FLOWER COLOR: Blue, pink, and lavender

BLOOM TIME: Spring and summer

FRAGRANCE: None

Clematis 'Vyvyan Pennell'

WHEN TO HARVEST: When the flower is a quarter to a half open

SPECIAL NEEDS: None

VASE LIFE: 7 to 10 days

Chionodoxa luciliae
Glory of the snow

FLOWER COLOR: Bright blue and light pink

BLOOM TIME: March

FRAGRANCE: None

WHEN TO HARVEST: When the first flower is open

SPECIAL NEEDS: None

VASE LIFE: 5 to 7 days

Chrysanthemum koreanum 'Sheffield'
Sheffield mum

FLOWER COLOR: Pink with a yellow eye

BLOOM TIME: Fall

FRAGRANCE: Spicy

WHEN TO HARVEST: When the flower is fully open

SPECIAL NEEDS: None

VASE LIFE: 2 to 3 weeks

Clematis cvs.
Clematis

FLOWER COLOR: Purple, blue, white, pink, red

BLOOM TIME: Spring, summer, and fall

FRAGRANCE: None

WHEN TO HARVEST: When the flower is open

SPECIAL NEEDS: Cut each flower on its own stem rather than cutting the vine.

VASE LIFE: 8 to 14 days

Cleome

Cleome hassleriana
Cleome, spider flower
FLOWER COLOR: White, pink, purple, and burgundy
BLOOM TIME: Late summer into fall
FRAGRANCE: Musky
WHEN TO HARVEST: When the flower is fully open
SPECIAL NEEDS: None
VASE LIFE: 6 to 8 days

Colchicum sp.
Autumn crocus
FLOWER COLOR: Lilac; 'Waterlily' is a double lilac; 'Album' is white.
BLOOM TIME: Fall
FRAGRANCE: None
WHEN TO HARVEST: Once the flower opens
SPECIAL NEEDS: Stems brown after a few days, so this flower is best in an opaque container. Its stems are too soft to poke into floral foam.
VASE LIFE: 4 to 6 days

Convallaria majalis
Lily-of-the-valley
FLOWER COLOR: White; 'Rosea' is pink.
BLOOM TIME: Spring
FRAGRANCE: Sweet-spicy
WHEN TO HARVEST: When half the bells are open, gently grasp the flowering stem at its base and pull up.
SPECIAL NEEDS: None
VASE LIFE: 4 or 5 days

Coreopsis verticillata
Tickseed
FLOWER COLOR: Yellow
BLOOM TIME: Early spring to late summer
FRAGRANCE: None
WHEN TO HARVEST: When flower is starting to open
SPECIAL NEEDS: None
VASE LIFE: 7 to 10 days

Corylopsis spicata
Spike winter hazel
FLOWER COLOR: Yellow
BLOOM TIME: Late winter, early spring
FRAGRANCE: Yes
WHEN TO HARVEST: In bud
SPECIAL NEEDS: None
VASE LIFE: 6 to 8 days

Cosmos bipinnatus
Cosmos
FLOWER COLOR: Yellow, orange, red, white, and pink to dark rose
BLOOM TIME: Summer through fall
FRAGRANCE: None
WHEN TO HARVEST: In colored bud stage or when first open before pollen forms
SPECIAL NEEDS: Floral preservative significantly extends its life.
VASE LIFE: 6 to 9 days

Crinum x powellii
Swamp lily
FLOWER COLOR: Pink; 'Album' is white.
BLOOM TIME: Summer
FRAGRANCE: Sweet scent akin to the sweet violet
WHEN TO HARVEST: When some of the blooms on the stalk are open
SPECIAL NEEDS: None
VASE LIFE: 7 to 10 days

Crocosmia cvs.
Montbretia
FLOWER COLOR: 'Lucifer' is red; 'Emily Mackenzie' has orange flowers with red centers.
BLOOM TIME: Midsummer until fall
FRAGRANCE: None
WHEN TO HARVEST: When first few buds show color; do not need to be open
SPECIAL NEEDS: None
VASE LIFE: 7 to 10 days

Crocus sp.
Crocus
FLOWER COLOR: White, blue, yellow, and purple
BLOOM TIME: Late winter, early spring
FRAGRANCE: Snow crocus have a sweet scent.
WHEN TO HARVEST: When the buds are colored
SPECIAL NEEDS: None
VASE LIFE: 3 to 5 days

Dahlia hybrids
Dahlia
FLOWER COLOR: White, pink, red, yellow, orange, and purple; in doubles and singles, large and small
BLOOM TIME: Summer through fall
FRAGRANCE: None
WHEN TO HARVEST: When fully open
SPECIAL NEEDS: None
VASE LIFE: 5 to 7 days

Dahlia

Delphinium hybrids
Delphinium, larkspur
FLOWER COLOR: Red, yellow, and blue
BLOOM TIME: Spring, summer
FRAGRANCE: None
WHEN TO HARVEST: When half to three-fourths of the flowers have opened
SPECIAL NEEDS: Immediately place in water with preservatives. Highly susceptible to ethylene, a gas given off by ripening fruit. Do not refrigerate near fruit.
VASE LIFE: 6 to 8 days

Dianthus barbatus
Sweet William
FLOWER COLOR: Rose, pink, red, white, salmon, and yellow
BLOOM TIME: May to June
FRAGRANCE: Sweet yet spicy
WHEN TO HARVEST: When 10 percent to 20 percent of flowers in the cluster are open
SPECIAL NEEDS: Cool temperatures are necessary for optimum performance and vase life.
VASE LIFE: 7 to 10 days

Dicentra spectabilis
Bleeding heart
FLOWER COLOR: Pink, red, white
BLOOM TIME: Spring
FRAGRANCE: None
WHEN TO HARVEST: When the heart-shaped flowers are fully formed
SPECIAL NEEDS: None
VASE LIFE: 4 or 5 days

Digitalis purpurea
Foxglove

FLOWER COLOR: Yellow, purple, and pink
BLOOM TIME: June to July
FRAGRANCE: None
WHEN TO HARVEST: When one-third of the lower flowers on the stem are open
SPECIAL NEEDS: All parts of the plants are poisonous, so handle with care.
VASE LIFE: 5 to 7 days

Echinacea purpurea
Purple coneflower

FLOWER COLOR: Purple, pink, rose, and white
BLOOM TIME: July to September
FRAGRANCE: None
WHEN TO HARVEST: When the flower is fully open
SPECIAL NEEDS: None
VASE LIFE: 7 to 10 days

Echinops bannaticus
Globe thistle

FLOWER COLOR: Blue
BLOOM TIME: Summer
FRAGRANCE: None
WHEN TO HARVEST: When half to three-fourths of the globe is bright blue
SPECIAL NEEDS: None
VASE LIFE: 6 to 12 days; it dries in the vase.

Eupatorium coelestinum
Hardy ageratum

FLOWER COLOR: White and purple
BLOOM TIME: Late summer through fall
FRAGRANCE: None
WHEN TO HARVEST: As soon as they open and pollen is visible
SPECIAL NEEDS: None
VASE LIFE: 7 to 10 days

Witch hazel

Forsythia x intermedia
Forsythia

FLOWER COLOR: Yellow
BLOOM TIME: Spring
FRAGRANCE: None
WHEN TO HARVEST: Branches with colorful flower buds can be forced. Cut as flowers begin to open.
SPECIAL NEEDS: None
VASE LIFE: 10 to 12 days

Galanthus nivalis
Snowdrop, fair maid of February

FLOWER COLOR: All cultivars are white. 'Flore Pleno' is double; *G. elwesii* has the largest flower.
BLOOM TIME: Mid- to late winter
FRAGRANCE: Sweet subtle
WHEN TO HARVEST: When its stem is full height, 6 to 10 inches
SPECIAL NEEDS: None
VASE LIFE: 5 to 7 days

Gladiolus sp.
Gladiola, sword lily, corn flag

FLOWER COLOR: Cream, blue, purple, pink, yellow, and red
BLOOM TIME: Midsummer to frost
FRAGRANCE: None

WHEN TO HARVEST: When one or two of the flowers on the stem are open
SPECIAL NEEDS: Tender plant; corms are dug up and stored indoors over winter.
VASE LIFE: 5 to 7 days

Hamamelis sp.
Witch hazel

FLOWER COLOR: Red, orange, and yellow
BLOOM TIME: Winter
FRAGRANCE: Curious, yet sweet, dusty exhalation like from an old medicine cabinet
WHEN TO HARVEST: When the tousled blooms are open
SPECIAL NEEDS: None
VASE LIFE: 5 to 7 days

Helianthus annuus
Sunflower

FLOWER COLOR: Shades of yellow, orange, red, and white
BLOOM TIME: Summer
FRAGRANCE: None
WHEN TO HARVEST: When almost open for pollenless forms, fully open otherwise
SPECIAL NEEDS: Varieties that do not produce pollen do not shed petals and live longer in the vase.
VASE LIFE: 7 to 9 days

Sunflower

Helleborus orientalis
Hellebore, Lenten rose

FLOWER COLOR: White flushed with pink, green, pink, or purple
BLOOM TIME: Late winter through late spring
FRAGRANCE: None
WHEN TO HARVEST: When stamens are visible
SPECIAL NEEDS: Sometimes the stems shrivel underwater and need to be recut and rehydrated in hot water.
VASE LIFE: 10 to 14 days

Hosta 'Royal Standard'
Hosta

FLOWER COLOR: White
BLOOM TIME: August through September
FRAGRANCE: Sweet
WHEN TO HARVEST: When the large buds are puffed and about to open
SPECIAL NEEDS: None
VASE LIFE: 7 to 10 days

Hyacinthoides sp.
Bluebell

FLOWER COLOR: Lavender blue
BLOOM TIME: Spring
FRAGRANCE: Sweet
WHEN TO HARVEST: When first bells open
SPECIAL NEEDS: None
VASE LIFE: 3 to 5 days

Hyacinthus orientalis
Hyacinth

FLOWER COLOR: Pinks, blues, white, yellow, purple, and salmon
BLOOM TIME: Spring
FRAGRANCE: Powerfully sweet
WHEN TO HARVEST: When most of the flowers are open
SPECIAL NEEDS: None
VASE LIFE: 7 to 10 days

Lacecap hydrangea

Hydrangea 'Annabelle'
Hydrangea

FLOWER COLOR: White for a month or so, then lime green

BLOOM TIME: Summer and fall

FRAGRANCE: None

WHEN TO HARVEST: To dry them, harvest when the flower is completely open and the petals feel leathery.

SPECIAL NEEDS: Immediately upon harvest, place stems in warm water.

VASE LIFE: 7 to 10 days; indefinitely dried

Hydrangea macrophylla
Lacecap and mophead hydrangeas

FLOWER COLOR: Blue, pink, or white

BLOOM TIME: Midsummer to late fall

FRAGRANCE: None

WHEN TO HARVEST: When the flower is completely open and the petals feel leathery

SPECIAL NEEDS: Immediately upon harvest, place stems in hot water (110°F to 120° F), then in a refrigerator. Do the same to revive wilted flowers.

VASE LIFE: 7 to 14 days; indefinitely dried

Iris hybrids
Bearded iris

FLOWER COLOR: Pink, blue, and white

BLOOM TIME: Summer

FRAGRANCE: Highly variable, from sweet to heavily sweet to sickeningly sweet like that of grape Kool-Aid; seek out varieties with wonderful scents, such as 'Beverly Sills', 'Lake Placid', and 'Banbury Ruffles'.

WHEN TO HARVEST: When one flower is open on the stem

SPECIAL NEEDS: Pick off fading flowers to enjoy the other blooms on the stem.

VASE LIFE: 1 to 3 days

Iris reticulata
Dwarf iris

FLOWER COLOR: Blue

BLOOM TIME: Late winter

FRAGRANCE: Similar to a violet

WHEN TO HARVEST: When the flower is fully open

SPECIAL NEEDS: None

VASE LIFE: 4 to 6 days

Lathyrus grandiflorus
Perennial sweet pea

FLOWER COLOR: Pink

BLOOM TIME: Summer

FRAGRANCE: None

WHEN TO HARVEST: When most of the flowers are open

SPECIAL NEEDS: None

VASE LIFE: 7 to 10 days

Lathyrus odoratus
Annual sweet pea

FLOWER COLOR: White, pink, blue, and lavender

BLOOM TIME: Spring

FRAGRANCE: Sweet and powerful

WHEN TO HARVEST: When two or three buds show color and stem is about a foot long

SPECIAL NEEDS: None

VASE LIFE: 5 to 7 days

Lavandula sp.
Lavender

FLOWER COLOR: Lavender

BLOOM TIME: Summer

FRAGRANCE: Yes

WHEN TO HARVEST: When half the flowers on the stem are half open

SPECIAL NEEDS: Hang upside down to dry.

VASE LIFE: 7 to 10 days

Leucanthemum x *superbum* (syn. *Chrysanthemum* x *superbum*)
Shasta daisy

FLOWER COLOR: White

BLOOM TIME: Summer into fall

FRAGRANCE: None

WHEN TO HARVEST: When the flower is starting to open

SPECIAL NEEDS: None

VASE LIFE: 7 to 10 days

Leucojum sp.
Snowflake

FLOWER COLOR: White

BLOOM TIME: Mid- to late spring

FRAGRANCE: None

WHEN TO HARVEST: When the top flowers on the stem are open

SPECIAL NEEDS: None

VASE LIFE: 7 to 10 days

Lilium oriental hybrids
Lily

FLOWER COLOR: Pink, white, yellow, orange, and red

BLOOM TIME: Summer

FRAGRANCE: Strong sweet floral

WHEN TO HARVEST: When at least two buds are colored and swollen

SPECIAL NEEDS: Pollen stains hands and clothes; handle carefully or remove the stamens.

VASE LIFE: 5 to 9 days

Lonicera sp.
Honeysuckle

FLOWER COLOR: Yellow, orange, coral, and bicolor

BLOOM TIME: Summer

FRAGRANCE: Hall's honeysuckle is wonderfully scented.

WHEN TO HARVEST: When the blooms are first open

SPECIAL NEEDS: None

VASE LIFE: 5 to 7 days

Lupinus perennis
Wild lupine

FLOWER COLOR: Blue

BLOOM TIME: Early summer

FRAGRANCE: Slightly sweet

WHEN TO HARVEST: When half the flowers on the spike are open

SPECIAL NEEDS: None

VASE LIFE: 5 to 7 days

Wild lupine

Matthiola incana
Stock

FLOWER COLOR: White, pink, red, and lavender

BLOOM TIME: Summer

FRAGRANCE: None

WHEN TO HARVEST: When half the flowers are open on the stem

SPECIAL NEEDS: If their stems are recut every few days, flower vase life is extended by 3 more days.

VASE LIFE: 7 to 10 days

Mertensia virginica
Virginia bluebells

FLOWER COLOR: Pink changing to blue

BLOOM TIME: Spring

FRAGRANCE: None

WHEN TO HARVEST: As soon as a few bells are open

SPECIAL NEEDS: Lasts longer if the stem features only flowers or only foliage

VASE LIFE: 2 to 4 days

Muscari armeniacum
Grape hyacinth

FLOWER COLOR: Blue

BLOOM TIME: Spring

FRAGRANCE: None

WHEN TO HARVEST: When blooms are half open

SPECIAL NEEDS: None

VASE LIFE: 5 to 7 days

Narcissus sp.
Daffodils

FLOWER COLOR: Yellow, pink, white, and orange

BLOOM TIME: Spring

FRAGRANCE: Many are heavily scented.

WHEN TO HARVEST: When fully open

SPECIAL NEEDS: Floral preservative is not needed, but change the water often.

VASE LIFE: 6 to 9 days

Garden phlox

Nicotiana sp.
Tobacco plant

FLOWER COLOR: *N. sylvestris* is white; *N. langsdorffii* is lime green; cultivars can be in many different colors.

BLOOM TIME: Summer and early fall

FRAGRANCE: *N. sylvestris* has a powerful perfume that gets stronger at night.

WHEN TO HARVEST: When flowers are open

SPECIAL NEEDS: None

VASE LIFE: 6 to 9 days

Nigella damascena
Love-in-a-mist

FLOWER COLOR: Blue

BLOOM TIME: Summer

FRAGRANCE: None

WHEN TO HARVEST: When flowers are colored but petals have not separated from the center

SPECIAL NEEDS: None

VASE LIFE: Flowers 7 to 10 days; seedpods indefinitely

Paeonia hybrids
Peony

FLOWER COLOR: White, pink, red

BLOOM TIME: Spring

FRAGRANCE: Many are heavily, sweetly scented

WHEN TO HARVEST: Once the bud is showing bright

color and petals can be seen

SPECIAL NEEDS: Immediately upon harvest, place stems in warm water to enhance water uptake.

VASE LIFE: 5 to 8 days

Paeonia lutea
Tree peony

FLOWER COLOR: Pink

BLOOM TIME: Spring

FRAGRANCE: Lemon-scented

WHEN TO HARVEST: When the flowers are open

SPECIAL NEEDS: None

VASE LIFE: 7 to 10 days

Phlox paniculata
Garden phlox

FLOWER COLOR: Lavender blue, white, pink, and rosy pink

BLOOM TIME: Midsummer to fall

FRAGRANCE: Sweet-scented, a little like baby powder

WHEN TO HARVEST: When half the flowers in a cluster are open

SPECIAL NEEDS: None

VASE LIFE: 5 to 7 days

Platycodon grandiflorus
Balloon flower

FLOWER COLOR: Blue, pink, and white

BLOOM TIME: Summer

FRAGRANCE: None

WHEN TO HARVEST: When two or three flowers on a stem are open

SPECIAL NEEDS: Pinch off dead blooms to extend vase life.

VASE LIFE: 5 to 8 days

Primula veris
Cowslip

FLOWER COLOR: Yellow

BLOOM TIME: Spring

FRAGRANCE: Sweet

WHEN TO HARVEST: When flowers are fully open

SPECIAL NEEDS: None

VASE LIFE: 4 to 6 days

Puschkinia scilloides
Striped squill

FLOWER COLOR: Faded denim blue

BLOOM TIME: Late winter, early spring

FRAGRANCE: None

WHEN TO HARVEST: When flowers are fully open

SPECIAL NEEDS: None

VASE LIFE: 4 to 6 days

Rosa sp. and hybrids
Rose

FLOWER COLOR: All colors except blue

BLOOM TIME: Summer to late fall

FRAGRANCE: None

WHEN TO HARVEST: While in bud

SPECIAL NEEDS: They last longer on shorter stems.

VASE LIFE: 5 to 10 days

Rose

Lilac 'Sensation'

Rudbeckia hirta
Black-eyed Susan
FLOWER COLOR: Yellow with a black center
BLOOM TIME: Summer into fall
FRAGRANCE: None
WHEN TO HARVEST: When the flower is open
SPECIAL NEEDS: None
VASE LIFE: 6 to 9 days

Salvia elegans
Pineapple sage
FLOWER COLOR: Red
BLOOM TIME: Fall
FRAGRANCE: Heavily pineapple-scented foliage
WHEN TO HARVEST: When half of the flowers on the spike are open
SPECIAL NEEDS: None
VASE LIFE: 7 to 10 days

Salvia farinacea
Sage
FLOWER COLOR: Bluish purple
BLOOM TIME: All summer and fall until hard frost
FRAGRANCE: None
WHEN TO HARVEST: When half of the flowers on the spike are open
SPECIAL NEEDS: None
VASE LIFE: 7 to 9 days; dries in the vase

Salvia leucantha
Mexican sage
FLOWER COLOR: Purple and white
BLOOM TIME: Late summer and fall
FRAGRANCE: Woodsy, burnt cocoa
WHEN TO HARVEST: When half of the flowers on the spike are open
SPECIAL NEEDS: None
VASE LIFE: 10 to 13 days; dries in the vase

Scilla siberica
Squill, scilla
FLOWER COLOR: Blue, white
BLOOM TIME: April
FRAGRANCE: None
WHEN TO HARVEST: When flowers are open
SPECIAL NEEDS: None
VASE LIFE: 5 to 7 days

Syringa vulgaris
Lilac
FLOWER COLOR: White, pink, and lavender
BLOOM TIME: Spring
FRAGRANCE: Heavy sweet
WHEN TO HARVEST: When half to two-thirds of the flowers are open
SPECIAL NEEDS: Remove foliage from flowering stem. Foliage has to be on a separate stem to last.
VASE LIFE: 3 to 5 days

Triteleia laxa 'Queen Fabiola'
Brodiaea, fool's onion
FLOWER COLOR: White, pink, and lavender
BLOOM TIME: Early summer
FRAGRANCE: None
WHEN TO HARVEST: When one of the many flowers opens on a stem
SPECIAL NEEDS: None
VASE LIFE: 10 to 14 days

Tropaeolum hybrids
Nasturtium
FLOWER COLOR: Yellow, orange, and crimson
BLOOM TIME: Summer
FRAGRANCE: Spicy
WHEN TO HARVEST: In bud or fully open
SPECIAL NEEDS: None
VASE LIFE: 5 to 7 days

Tulipa hybrids
Tulip
FLOWER COLOR: All colors
BLOOM TIME: Spring
FRAGRANCE: Several, such as 'Ballerina', 'Orange Favorite', 'Peach Blossom', and 'Shirley', are sweetly scented.
WHEN TO HARVEST: When the entire bud is colored
SPECIAL NEEDS: Flowers bend toward the light.
VASE LIFE: 6 to 10 days

Verbena bonariensis
Brazilian verbena
FLOWER COLOR: Purple
BLOOM TIME: Summer until late fall
FRAGRANCE: None
WHEN TO HARVEST: When flower cluster is open
SPECIAL NEEDS: None
VASE LIFE: 7 to 10 days; often dries in the vase

Zinnia

Vitex agnus-castus
Chaste tree
FLOWER COLOR: Purple
BLOOM TIME: Late summer into mid-fall
FRAGRANCE: Light spicy
WHEN TO HARVEST: When fully open
SPECIAL NEEDS: None
VASE LIFE: 7 to 10 days; often dries in the vase

Wisteria sp.
Wisteria
FLOWER COLOR: White and lavender
BLOOM TIME: Spring
FRAGRANCE: Sweetly strong scent
WHEN TO HARVEST: When the first blooms open
SPECIAL NEEDS: The shorter the stem, the longer it lasts.
VASE LIFE: 5 to 7 days

Zinnia elegans
Zinnia
FLOWER COLOR: Many colors and bicolors
BLOOM TIME: Summer
FRAGRANCE: None
WHEN TO HARVEST: When the flower is open and the center is tight
SPECIAL NEEDS: The stems are hollow; snip carefully, so they don't collapse.
VASE LIFE: 7 to 10 days

Sources

For more garden bouquet ideas, go to suzybalesgarden.com.

Afloral.com
afloral.com
1-888-299-4100

- Bouquet holders
- Pointed base candle cups
- Oasis
- Netted spheres: 4.5 inches
- Floral foam cones
- Floral foam wreaths: 8.5, 12, and 15 inches
- Wire picks, wire pins, and wire wreath forms
- Water tubes and picks
- Glass cube vases

Chain of Life Network
chainoflifenetwork.org
Information on postharvest handling of flowers is constantly being updated on this Web site.

English Creek Gardens
englishcreekgardens.com
1-800-610-8610

- Topiary forms
- Tussie mussies
- Victorian vase pins

mainewreathco.com
mainewreathco.com
1-877-846-3797

- Wire wreath frames: circles, squares, snowflakes, stars
- Wire
- Fresh greens
- Floral foam

Michaels
michaels.com
Web site is for locating stores and products; products not available for sale online.

- Oasis
- Wire and wire wreath forms
- Floral tape and adhesives
- Pointed base candle cups
- Vases
- Grapevine wreath forms
- Moss, ribbons, baskets

Omni Farm
omnifarm.com
1-800-873-3327

- Fraser fir and white pine garlands
- Undecorated wreaths
- Wreath hangers

Pier 1 Imports
pier1.com
Great source for vases and baskets. Web site is for locating stores and products; products not available for sale online.

Save-on-crafts
save-on-crafts.com
1-831-768-8428

- Floral netting, 12 inches x 48 inches
- Oasis netted floral foam spheres, 6 inches
- Oasis
- Oasis floral foam wreaths
- Floral cages with Oasis
- Bouquet holders
- Floral tape
- Pointed base candle holders
- Floral sticky clay
- Ribbon
- Chandeliers
- Vase gems
- Glass cube vases
- Wreath hangers

VivaTerra
vivaterra.com
1-800-233-6011

- Twig centerpiece

TO ALL MY FRIENDS

I am grateful to all of the many people who helped me with this book. Allan M. Armitage, a professor of horticulture at the University of Georgia, did research for the cut-flower industry on when to harvest flowers and how to extend their vase life. Together with Judy M. Laushman, he published his results in the book *Specialty Cut Flowers* (Timber Press, 2003). I am indebted to them both for the information on when to harvest and how to prolong the bloom of many popular flowers. In addition, I thank Allan for his continuing friendship and collaboration. He graciously wrote the foreword. I can only aspire to be as good as he claims I am.

Barbara Winkler suggested the book's title and was the first person to read the text and help me shape it. As always, Gina Norgard is both my right hand and my left hand. She jumped in to help with photo shoots, research, and anything else that needed doing. Doug Turshen created the design of the book and his assistant, David Huang, laid it out. They both put in many hours trying to fit in all of the pictures and helping me to shrink the text. I thank them for their hard work and attention to detail.

Steven Randazzo has a wonderful eye and is a talented photographer. He photographed most of the pictures in the book. Steven often worked long days photographing my arrangements. His assistant, Jonathan Hoener, was delightful company and a great help. Robert Starkoff, Richard Warren, and Michael Luppino have worked with me on many shoots for *Family Circle* magazine. I thank them for letting me include some of our earlier work together here. Bridget Gallagher took beautiful pictures at my daughter's wedding. She graciously sent me one to include in this book.

J. Barry Ferguson, a friend of 20 years and a renowned flower designer, shared many of his techniques with me. He designed the candle cup on page 115 and the garland on page 187. His former assistant, Tracy Vivona, now owns T. Alexandra, a floral business. She, too, has shared her techniques and equipment to help me with this book.

Karen Bolesta and Nancy N. Bailey, the editorial team at Rodale, are thoughtful, smart, supportive, and easy to work with. They had many excellent ideas and

helped at every step along the way. I am grateful to them as well.

I am indebted to Steve Murphy and Karen Rinaldi for acquiring the book. I hope they are as pleased with this book as I am, but that is probably unrealistic.

Last but not least, I thank my husband, Carter F. Bales, for his encouragement, support, and love, even when I'm not in the best of moods.

To all of my friends noted above, I hope the joy of flowers keeps on enriching your lives.

INDEX

Boldface page numbers indicate photographs. <u>Underscored</u> references indicate boxed text, tables or charts.